TEN HOUSES

TEN HOUSES

Edited by Oscar Riera Ojeda

Wheeler Kearns Architects

First published in the United States of America by:

Rockport Publishers, Inc.

33 Commercial Street

Gloucester, Massachusetts 01930

Telephone: 978-282-9590

Fax: 978-283-2742

Distributed to the book trade and art trade in the United States of America by

North Light Books, an imprint of F & W Publications

1504 Dana Avenue

Cincinnati, Ohio 45207

Telephone: 513-531-2222

Other distribution by

Rockport Publishers Inc.

ISBN 1-56496-493-0

10 9 8 7 6 5 4 3 2 1

Printed in Hong Kong

Cover Photograph: Essex Residence and Office. Photograph by William Kildow

Back Cover Photographs are of projects on pages (from left, top to bottom) 16, 26, 38, 44, 56, 70, 80, 88, 102, 110

Page 2: Photograph: Mussman Residence. Photograph by George Lambros

Graphic Design: Lucas H. Guerra / Oscar Riera Ojeda
Layout: Oscar Riera Ojeda
Composition: Hunha Lee

Contents

Foreword

by Rodolphe el-Khoury

After Robert Venturi's caustic "less is a bore," along with other polemical assaults by architects and critics, Mies van der Rohe's works epitomized the dogma and limitations of Modernism. For a whole generation of architects interested in complexity and contradiction, in regional accents, vernacular idioms, and popular culture, Mies' American buildings, such as the pavilions of the IIT campus in Chicago, seemed much too self-referential and anemic to engage the multicultural challenge of the contemporary city.

The Miesian virtues that had driven the Modern movement in America became liabilities: the intransigent integrity of the formal language, the rigor and calculated austerity of the composition, the rationalized geometry and homogeneity of the structure were all at odds with the postmodern predilection for irony and hybrid constructions, for the formless and the baroque. The aspiration to a universal architectural language—the credo of Modernism since the Enlightenment—became particularly suspect, especially when the "universal" was tailored to the ideals of the white male.

Despite such critical hostility, some aspects of Mies' work continue to flourish. A recent exhibition at the Museum of Modern Art showcased several variations on Miesian themes: instances of contemporary experiments in glass architecture, transparency, and "Light Constructions" where the curtain wall features most prominently.

But if the Miesian brand of Modernism is still relevant to contemporary architectural practice, its influence has to be sought beyond the benign fetishization of curtain wall, glass and steel, at a more constitutive register of architectural theory and practice. The work of Wheeler Kearns Architects would be a good place to start. The legacy of Mies, say in the Bohan Kemp Residence, may not be as overt as the literal quotations now found in the mannerist revival of the International Style. In fact, the pitched roof—not to mention the vernacular inspiration—is reason enough to discredit the Miesian pedigree. Yet this building's affinity with the Farnsworth House is unmistakable. The affinity is conceptual more than formal: it is due to shared principles in the conception and rationalization of space and structure.

Wheeler Kearns Architects does not follow such principles with intent on recreating the Miesian look. The investment, rather, is in the genuine expansion of the means and scope of modern architecture to meet the demands and build the aspirations of a rapidly changing culture.

Rodolphe el-Khoury is an architect, critic, and historian who teaches at the Harvard Graduate School of Design.

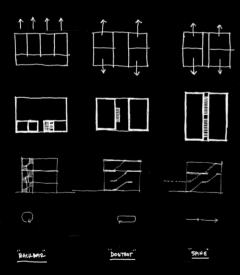

Left: *Mussman Residence, concept diagrams.*
Opposite Page: *Project for Wheeler House,*
Chicago Illinois, 1989. Floor Plans and Elevations.

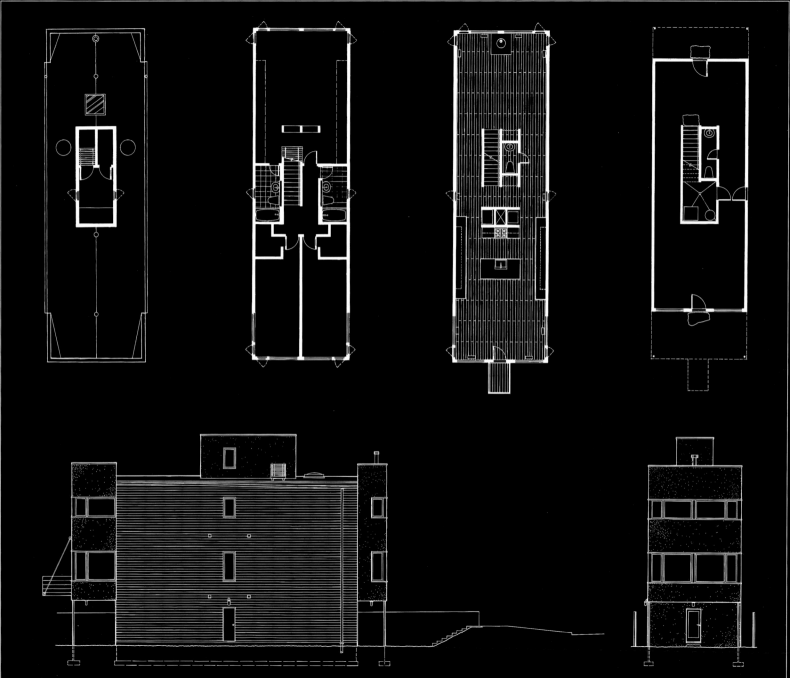

Introduction

by Thomas H. Beeby

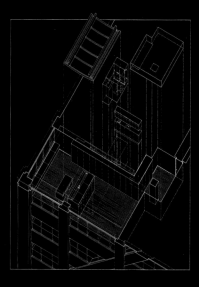

Final success will depend on the skill of the leaders to combine their forces to work as a team, being convinced that the team is greater than any of its individual members. It is that spirit, not hero worship, which makes for the climate in which cultural refinement in our democracy will grow. Its influence will be deeper than any isolated individual effort can be, since its products go through the acid test of being checked and re-checked by all participants of the team.

—Walter Gropius, April 17, 1950, Blackstone Hotel, Chicago

One of the lesser publicized events in Chicago architectural history occurred at the Blackstone Hotel during the celebration of the addition of the Institute of Design to the Illinois Institute of Technology. At this occasion two of the primary contesting progeny of the German Bauhaus were re-united in one institution on South State Street in Chicago. The renowned IIT architectural program— under the sober and steady hand of Mies Van Der Rohe—joined the equally influential Institute of Design, founded by Lazlo Moholy-Nagy. Both soon were to be housed in a sublime enclosure designed by Mies.

Three primary speeches were presented on that day. Serge Chermeyeff, the institute's director, spoke at length about the new and productive alliances being forged by the architectural community in America with the industrialists who were eager to produce new technologies and processes hardly imagined before the war. He noted the significance that the coupling of Mies' and Moholy's legacies would have on the evolution of American architecture.

Walter Gropius from Harvard spoke of the importance of teamwork within the design world as the key to the success of the New Architecture. He stressed the value of assembling teams of informed specialists who could produce highly

Left and Opposite Page: Wine merchant's studio, 47th floor of John Hancock Tower, Chicago, Illinois, 1996. A continuous wall of cabinetry absorbs and completely conceals the bath, kitchen, and dressing storage in this large room—converted from an existing apartment—for overnight guests and private office functions. Kept clear of obstructions, the north and west window walls capitalize on the dramatic skyline views.

integrated work—in contrast to the lonely genius searching for inspiration—an attitude certainly endorsed by the Institute of Design.

The final talk was offered by Mies Van Der Rohe, who spoke of the importance of architecture to culture. He suggested that the ultimate goal of architecture, although based on sound construction, was to satisfy the soul of society through the revelation of spiritual truth. Thus was laid the foundation stone of the composite belief system that drove Chicago architecture for the next quarter century. Although the participants in this ceremony appear to be in sympathetic accord, the discord between competing personalities prohibited any further collaboration in a real sense.

Inadvertently, Wheeler Kearns has reinvented the optimism of that fateful day at the Blackstone when the Bauhaus was momentarily reborn in Chicago. The participants in the firm steadfastly pursue the principles laid down that day in a manner that is purposeful and resolute. They also display some of the curious but interesting discontinuities of thought occurring when one moves conceptually from Chermeyeff to Gropius to Mies.

The first and most profoundly positive aspect of the firm of Wheeler Kearns is its organization and modus operandi. It is one of the few genuine group architectural practices at work today in this country. Totally democratic and open in their manner of work, much like the Institute of Design, there is little pride of individual authorship at work among the members of the firm. They exhaustively discuss, criticize, and agonize over each project. This arduous process creates buildings that are conceptually strong and technically advanced; as Gropius insisted, an informed group working in concert can create product that surpasses the limitations of one mind. Interestingly the work of the firm avoids any

Opposite Page: Fullerton Residence, Chicago, Illinois, 1988. A large townhouse on a dense urban site had a very dark interior. The entire structure was transformed by carving a four-story interior "courtyard" out of the volume. The result is a more formal front house connected by bridges to the

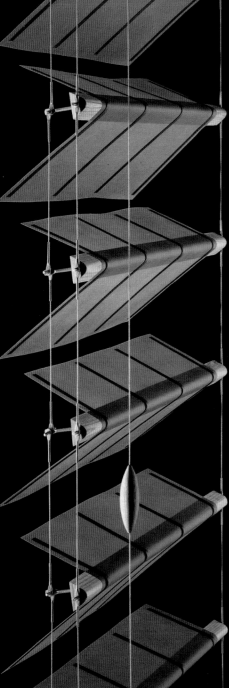

tendency toward homogeneous product, through careful policing followed by critical intervention. This control prevents lack of focus that is sometimes found in the work of group practices.

A second characteristic of the work of Wheeler Kearns is its belief that current technology helps produce high-quality work through an analytical process that raises the ordinary to the unique. In the manner of the Institute of Design, the firm searches for ways to appropriate analogous techniques and systems from similar disciplines for its own use. In the process Wheeler Kearns has produced a series of small structures that borrow elements and methods from larger typologies of building with great skill and understanding. A related mindset has also allowed the architects to borrow forms related to simple vernacular building, an enterprise that has always been seductive for Modernists. However, this aspect of the work of the firm would probably be frowned upon by the three particular Modernists who spoke at the Blackstone that day. Certainly all three would have approved the remodelings completed by the firm that display unusual intelligence in their transformation of nineteenth-century houses into twentieth-century constructs of abstract beauty while losing none of their sense of dwelling.

This brings the discussion to the relation between Mies and the work of Wheeler Kearns. There is a tidy, formal aspect to its architecture that clearly relates to the large commercial firms such as Skidmore Owings and Merrill— one of Mies' successors—where some of the group received their training. Based on the clarity of Miesian planning (which must find its roots in 19th Century Neo-Classicism), much of the work of these earlier firms had a

Left and Right: Conceptual translucent screen, 1992. Asked by Formica Corporation to propose creative uses of their plastic laminate product, Wheeler Kearns Architects chose to investigate its inherent material properties. Warm, translucent light filtering through the Formica backing material inspired the creation of a light-modulating screen.
Opposite Page: (Far Right) Astor Street Residence, Chicago Illinois, 1997. Seeking to gather as much light as possible in a dense urban site, a glass pavilion was added to the rear of a noteworthy 1890s Arts and

formulaic aspect void of critical interest. This is not the most productive Chicago legacy inherited by Wheeler Kearns, but it does inform the practice. I would maintain however that the best work of Wheeler Kearns rises to engage Mies directly in a truly profound way. Here the firm's reductive aesthetic speaks to matters of genuine human perception and changes one's understanding of the world. The members of the firm enter into a dialogue with that other great Miesian tradition, that of individual Chicago architects in pursuit of the spiritual truth through reductive means of spatial organization accompanied by constructional virtuosity. They join the worthy company of Keck, Goldsmith, Haid, Takeuchi, and Krueck, to name only a few. This lesser acclaimed strain of Chicago architecture follows a path that has considerable risk, for it requires perfection in order to succeed. The fact that Wheeler Kearns Architects has expanded its formal vocabulary beyond that of Mies further complicates its mission. It is with great interest that I watch its current work and try to anticipate the next building.

Finally, I believe the work displayed in this book represents a continuing struggle by Wheeler Kearns to produce an architecture of true significance. The firm's members are becoming genuine heirs to those who spoke in Chicago that historic day forty years ago. Although that position is not necessarily their stated intent, it is clear they are following that path in their best work, although the terrain they traverse is considerably altered by time.

I hope you will understand that architecture has nothing to do with the inventions of forms. It is not a playground for children, young or old. Architecture is the real battleground of the spirit.

—*Mies van der Rohe, April 17, 1950, Blackstone Hotel, Chicago*

Thomas Hall Beeby is an internationally recognized practicing architect, teacher, and critic. A principal in the Chicago firm Hammond Beeby and Babka since 1971, he received his undergraduate degree from Cornell University and his graduate degree from Yale University. After teaching for many years at the Illinois Institute of Technology, Beeby served as Director of Architecture at the University of Illinois at Chicago and as Dean of the School of Architecture at Yale, where he now teaches as an adjunct professor. Mr. Beeby has won many national awards and served as a distinguished participant on many design juries, panels, and publications. His major projects include the Rice Pavilion at the Art Institute of Chicago, and two libraries in Chicago: the Conrad Sulzer Regional Library, and the Harold Washington Library.

Opposite Page and bottom: Wilson Painting Studio, Chicago, Illinois, 1993. Reclaiming a burned-out storefront with a surrounding garden, three spaces were created: a symmetrical front room receives guests; the center space serves as a warren for utilities; and in the large space the artist paints in a corner beneath the skylight.

Below: *Seminary Street Residences, Chicago Illinois, 1991. These two town houses complement each other. The corner house is lower and outward-looking, with an emphasis on cantilevered corner bays. The adjacent house turns inward and extends upward to capture south light within a central court.*

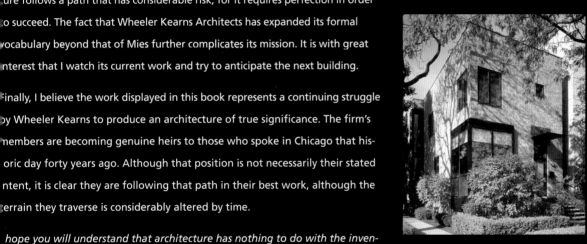

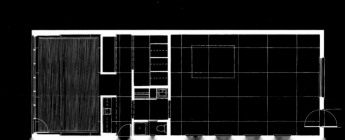

Bohan Kemp Residence

Buchanan Township, Michigan

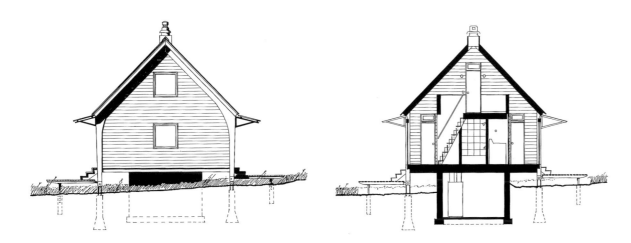

Sited just beyond the tree line where a stand of pines breaks and meadow begins, this house is approached on foot through rows of mature pines. A long platform—elevated upon pilotis to minimize the impact to the site both visually and environmentally—maximizes the experience of these two simultaneous landscapes.

Sharing roots with local Michiana polebarns, this economical structure of glue-laminated Douglas fir bents, braces, and decking stands on galvanized steel stirrups, keeping it clear of runoff and snow. Two small, concrete mechanical cores with baths above anchor the central space at both ends. Above the baths, small lofts overlook the central living space. Whole-house fans, coupled with transom windows, keep the tall volume well-ventilated during the summer. Protected under deep eaves of corrugated steel, generous decks and windows maximize connections to the two landscapes.

Above: *Approaching the house through a stand of pine trees planted in a grid, the horizontal sweep of the floor and roof structure counters the verticality of the trees and forms a visual gateway to the meadow beyond.*

Opposite Page: *The structure and its elevated viewing platform sit gently on the sloping terrain. The building's visual transparency emphasizes the contrast between the warm interior palette and the subdued gray of the exterior.*

South Elevation

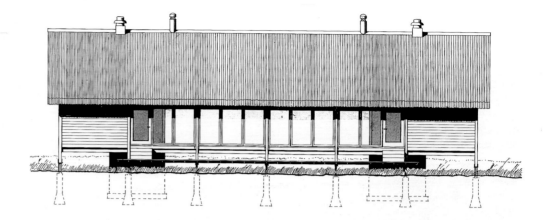

Floor Plan

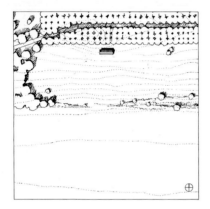

Site Plan

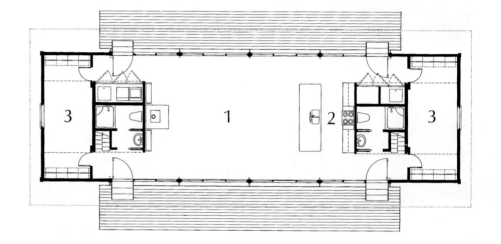

1. Living / Dining
2. Kitchen
3. Bedroom

Longitudinal Section

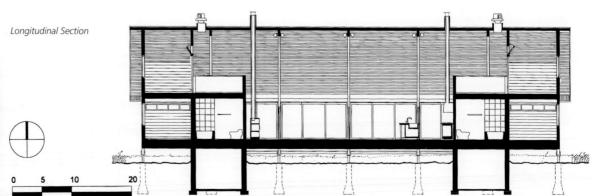

0   5   10   20

Opposite Page: The exploded axonometric drawing illustrates the wooden glue-laminated bents and beams as an expressed armature for the building. Walls and windows are infilled between the structure, and the wood-plank roof decking and corrugated metal finish roofing shelters the entire construction. The light fixtures (photos, far right) punctuate the rhythm of the structure during evening hours.

Right: The roof extends over the porch decks with the aid of galvanized steel brackets bolted to the glue-laminated structure.

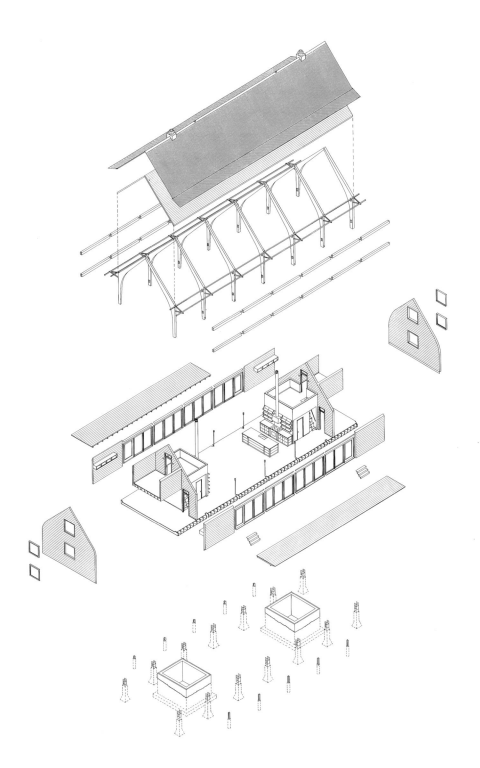

The simple, practical materials were chosen because of their strong relationship to the site. The exterior grays through the seasons in deference to the colors of nature; the interior glows with warmth. The exterior palette consists of stained shiplap cedar, galvanized roofing and trim, weathered decks, and expressed structural ribs. Inside, Douglas fir serves as the predominant interior material, used for structural bents, wall siding, ceiling decking, cabinets, and shelves. The natural linoleum floors, painted gypsum board, and blackened-steel-and-aluminum frames temper the fir's natural warmth.

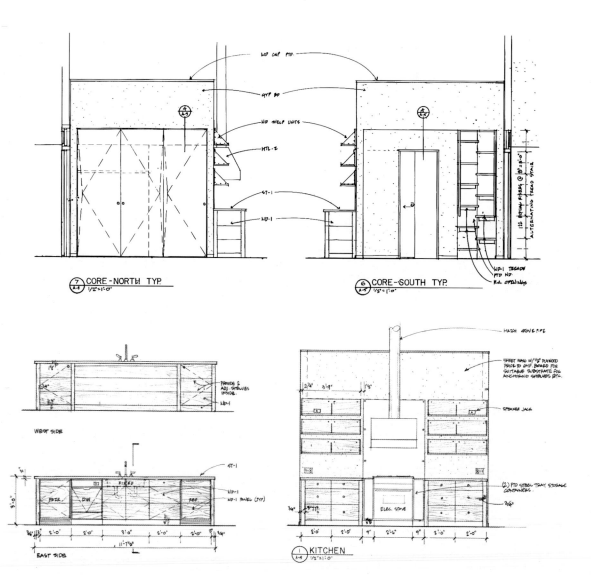

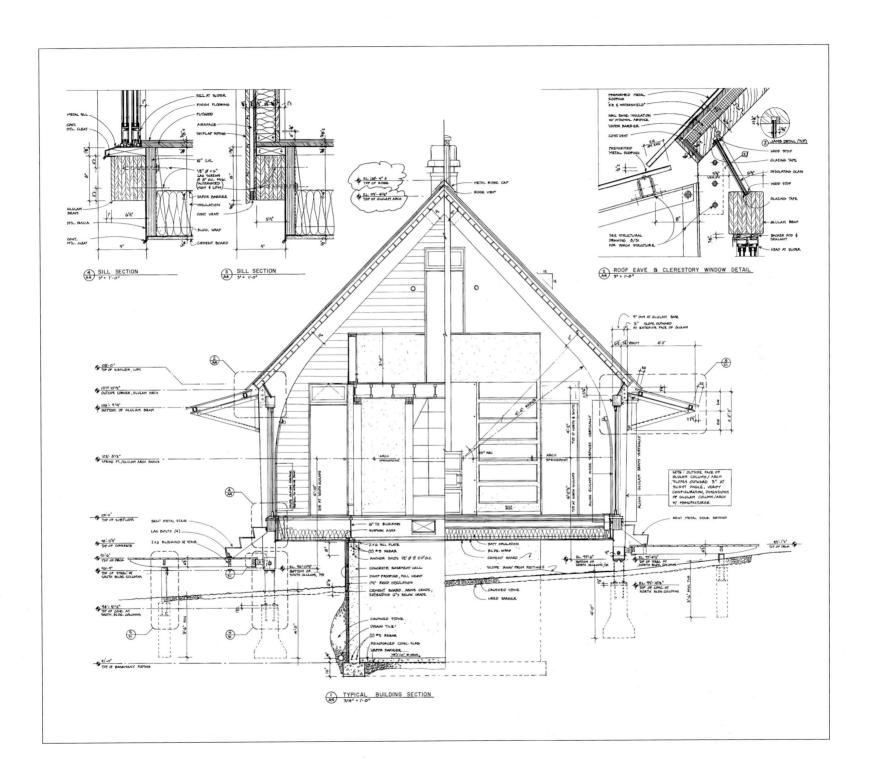

SILL AT SLIDER
FINISH FLOORING
PLYWOOD
AIRSPACE
SHIPLAP SIDING

METAL SILL
CONT. MTL. CLEAT

16" LVL
1/2" Ø x 6" LAG SCREWS @ 8" O.C. MIN. (ALTERNATED HIGH & LOW)

VAPOR BARRIER
INSULATION
CONT. VENT

GLULAM BEAM

MTL. FASCIA
CONT. MTL. CLEAT

BLDG. WRAP
CEMENT BOARD

④ SILL SECTION
A4 3" = 1'-0"

③ SILL SECTION
A4 3" = 1'-0"

EL. 108'-4" ±
TOP OF RIDGE

EL. 107'-4½" ±
TOP OF GLULAM ARCH

METAL RIDGE CAP
RIDGE VENT

PREFORMED METAL ROOFING
ICE & WATERSHIELD
NAIL BASE INSULATION W/ INTEGRAL AIRSPACE
VAPOR BARRIER
CONT VENT
PREFORMED METAL ROOFING

② JAMB DETAIL (TYP)

WOOD STOP
GLAZING TAPE
INSULATING GLASS
WOOD STOP
GLAZING TAPE

GLULAM BEAM
BACKER ROD & SEALANT
HEAD AT SLIDER

SEE STRUCTURAL DRAWING S/51 FOR PORCH STRUCTURE

② ROOF EAVE & CLERESTORY WINDOW DETAIL
A4 3" = 1'-0"

108'-0"
TOP OF SUBFLOOR, LOFT

107'-10½"
OUTSIDE CORNER, GLULAM ARCH

106'-9½"
BOTTOM OF GLULAM BEAM

103'-8½"
SPRING PT./GLULAM ARCH RADIUS

100'-0"
TOP OF SUBFLOOR

98'-6¾"
TOP OF CONC.STB

96'-6"
TOP OF DECK

96'-4"
TOP OF STEEL AT SOUTH BLDG. COLUMNS

94'-5½"
TOP OF CONC. AT SOUTH. BLDG. COLUMNS

91'-0"
TOP OF BASEMENT FOOTING

BENT METAL STAIR
LAG BOLTS (4)
2x6 BLOCKING AT STAIR

EL. 99'-10½"
BOTTOM OF SOUTH GLULAMS, TYP.

ARCH SPRINGPOINT

85° ARC

ARCH SPRINGPOINT

16" TJI BLOCKING
SIMPSON A35F

2x6 SILL PLATE
(2) #5 REBAR
ANCHOR BOLTS ½" Ø @ 2'-0 O.C.
CONCRETE BASEMENT WALL
DAMP PROOFING, FULL HEIGHT
1½" RIGID INSULATION
CEMENT BOARD, ABOVE GRADE, EXTENDING 6"± BELOW GRADE

CRUSHED STONE
DRAIN TILE
(2) #5 REBAR
REINFORCED CONC. SLAB
VAPOR BARRIER
¼"/10" TO DRAIN

9" DIM AT GLULAM. BASE
3" SLOPE OUTWARD AT EXTERIOR FACE OF GLULAM

VERIFY   4'-8"

NOTE: OUTSIDE FACE OF GLULAM COLUMN / ARCH SLOPES OUTWARD 3" AT SLIGHT ANGLE. VERIFY CONFIGURATION, DIMENSIONS OF GLULAM COLUMN / ARCH W/ MANUFACTURER.

BENT METAL STAIR BEYOND

BATT INSULATION
BLDG. WRAP
CEMENT BOARD
SLOPE AWAY FROM FOOTINGS

EL. 97'-0"
BOTTOM OF NORTH GLULAMS, TYP.

EL. 97'-4½"
TOP OF STEEL AT NORTH BLDG. COLUMNS

93'-1½"
TOP OF DECK

EL. 95'-10½"
TOP OF CONC. AT NORTH BLDG. COLUMNS

CRUSHED STONE
WEED BARRIER

① TYPICAL BUILDING SECTION
A4 3/4" = 1'-0"

LaPoint Residence

Buchanan Township, Michigan

B efore construction on this elevated wooded plateau in southwestern Michigan, the owners of this house approached Wheeler Kearns Architects with a modest budget, expressing a desire: a retreat-like atmosphere with simple modern spaces. The program is concise; bedrooms below and an open living space lifted above. Because the owners could not afford a separate screened porch, the communal space essentially became one, with views in all directions. In the winter, the surrounding trees shed their leaves and reveal a cornfield to the north and a lake to the south visible through a thicket of tree trunks.

Means of construction were kept very simple. A two-story, rigid moment-frame rests on a shallow "slab on grade" foundation. The upper floor utilizes plywood web joists fifty-two feet (sixteen meters) long, which run the long direction of the house. The joists provide greater efficiencies of construction as well as the stiffness of continuous spans over interior supporting walls. Top chord hung trusses support the roof while providing an internal lighting cove. The continuous envelope of off-the-shelf sliding glass doors on the second floor establishes a disciplined module for the overall dimensions. The only interruptions of the view are created by structural steel shear walls that form the backdrop for freestanding fireplaces at both ends. The changing seasons, light, and landscape become part of the architectural experience in a house separated from—yet integrated with—its surroundings, fulfilling the client's desire to live amongst the trees.

Above: The house seen from the road below to the southwest.

Opposite Page: The ground-floor bedrooms receive light and ventilation from the sides, reducing the entry elevation to an elemental expression of access with elevated living space.

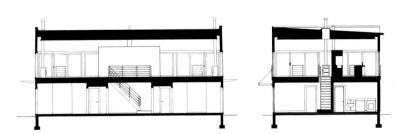

South Elevation

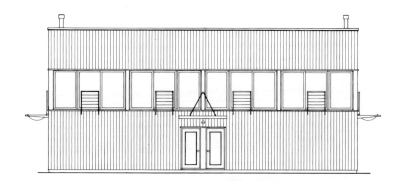

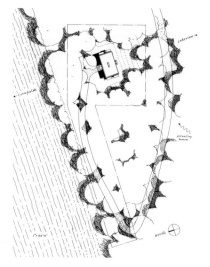

Site Plan

Second Floor Plan

1. Entry
2. Bedroom
3. Utility
4. Living / Dining
5. Kitchen

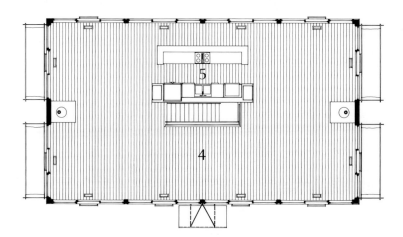

First Floor Plan

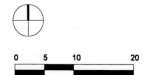

0   5   10   20

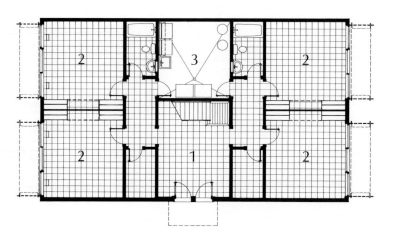

Opposite Page: *To keep costs within budget, the modules of the structural bay and the sliding glass doors are coordinated for maximum efficiency and strictly maintained.*

Left: *The primary structure uses built-up micro-lam columns and beams, with embedded steel plates at the joints to form a structurally rigid moment-frame. Second floor structure runs fifty-two feet (sixteen meters) in the long direction. Roof trusses span the opposite short direction for structural efficiency.*

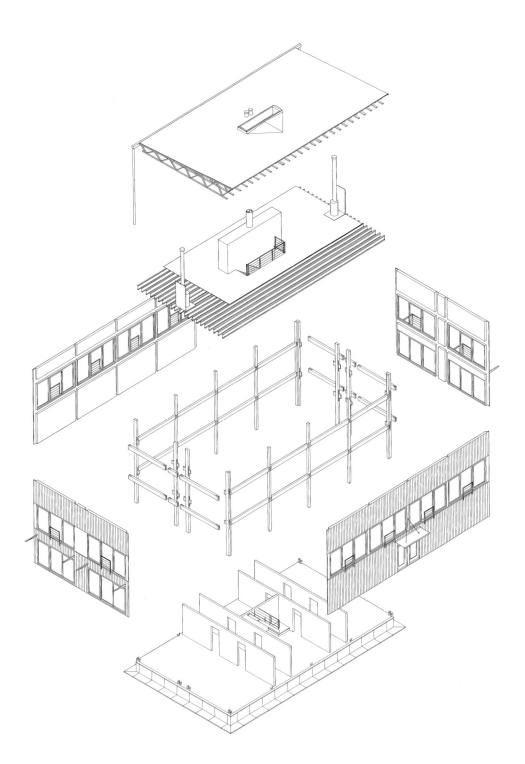

Above: Entry hall stair to the upper living spaces. Tiled in a cool slate, the first level features a pad of wood dropping down into the foyer as an offering of the warmth above.

Opposite Page: One ascends the stair alongside a blue mass, which terminates short of the celling. At the top of the stair the expansive view of trees all around reveals itself. The physical warmth provided by wood stoves at either end of the space echoes the warm color of the southern yellow pine flooring.

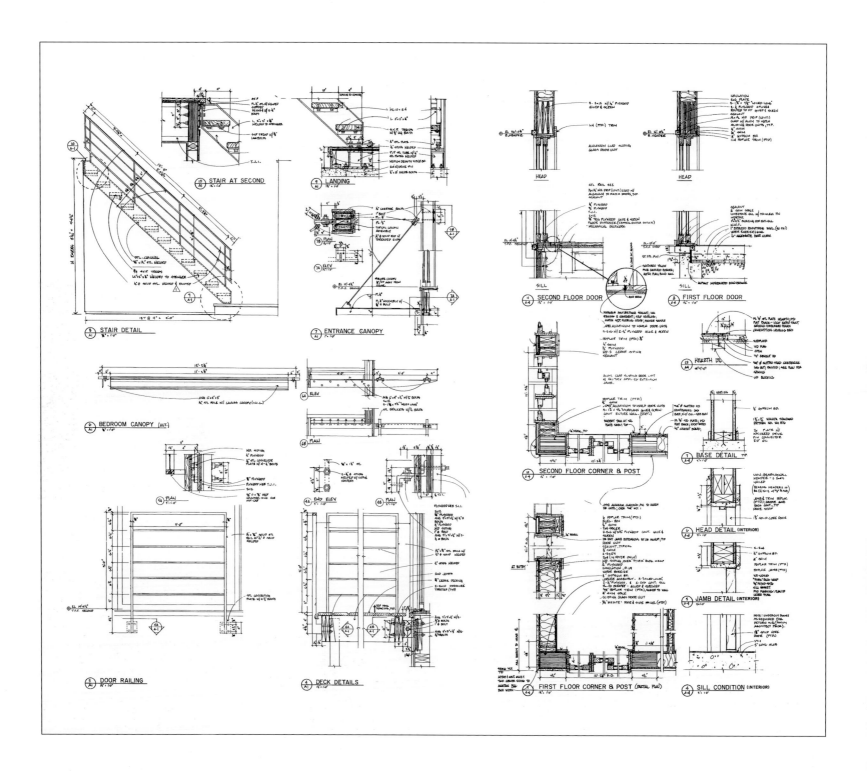

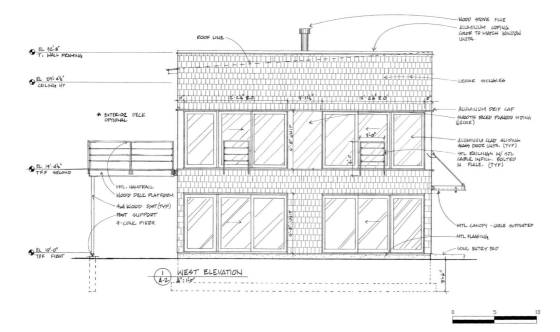

EL 32'-8"
T. WALL FRAMING

EL 29'-4½"
CEILING HT

* EXTERIOR DECK
OPTIONAL

EL 19'-4½"
T.F.F SECOND

MTL. HANDRAIL
WOOD DECK PLATFORM
4x4 WOOD POST (TYP)
POST SUPPORT
3-CONC PIERS.

EL 10'-0"
T.F.F FIRST

WOOD STOVE FLUE
ALUMINUM COPING
COLOR TO MATCH WINDOW
UNITS

CEDAR SHINGLES

ROOF LINE

ALUMINUM DRIP CAP
SMOOTH FACED PLYWOOD SIDING
(CEDAR)

ALUMINUM CLAD SLIDING
GLASS DOOR UNITS. (TYP)
STL RAILINGS W/ STL
CABLE INFILL. BOLTED
IN PLACE. (TYP)

MTL CANOPY - CABLE SUPPORTED

MTL FLASHING

CONC ENTRY PAD

① WEST ELEVATION
A-2   ⅛"=1'-0"

0   5   10

2-WOOD STOVE FLUES

ALUM. COPING
COLOR TO MATCH
SLIDING DOORS.

CEDAR SHINGLES

ALUMINUM DRIP
CAP.
ALUMINUM CLAD
SLIDING GLASS
DOOR UNITS (TYP)

STL RAILINGS W/
STL CABLE INFILL
BOLTED IN PLACE
(TYP)

MTL. CANOPY
(CABLE SUPPORTED)
LIGHT

CONC ENTRY PAD

MTL FLASHING

EL - 32'-6"
T. FRAMING

CEILING

EL 19'-4½"
T.F.F SECOND

EL 10'-0"
T.F.F FIRST

① SOUTH ELEVATION
A-1   ⅛"=1'-0"

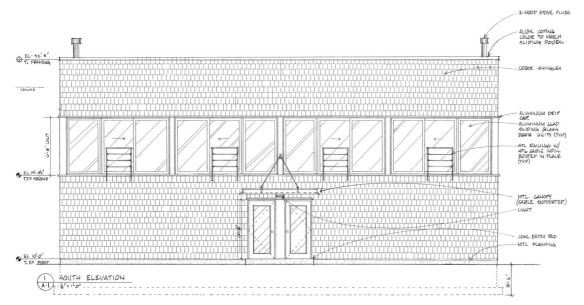

Michigan Residence

Buchanan Township, Michigan

hrough dense woods and atop a plateau, this house sits in a small clearing. The characteristic feature of the site is the differing landscape one sees looking in the four cardinal directions. The few requirements for the house: simple geometry; a relaxed atmosphere; and a large gathering space. The project developed from a four-square house previously proposed for the site by Wheeler Kearns Architects, which was not executed. Its primary feature of a compact, cubic volume with equal emphasis in the four cardinal directions was retained, but the spirit of the form was shifted from a stately farmhouse vernacular to a more ambitious contemporary re-interpretation of form that refers to— while it transforms—the prototype of the Palladian "Villa Rotunda." The Palladian centered, figural void and dense periphery is inverted to a dense figural center with a sparse periphery and voided corners. The communal spaces are clustered in a single large room punctured by a central spiral stair. The result is an overall spatial emphasis projected out into the landscape and anchored around the central core. The varying landscapes in the four cardinal directions are acknowledged with an alternating set of screen porches and entry vestibules.

Steel-frame construction allows for bedrooms, windows, and doors to continue the voided corner theme throughout. Paired second-floor bedroom doors combine with all-glass corner windows, eliminating corner visual obstructions.

Above and Below: The previously proposed four-square house for the site was a product of the Camp Madron House types (pages 110–119). The four-square planning concepts were retained but the architects pursued a more contemporary expression of form.

Opposite Page: The completed project design put greater emphasis on panoramic views from the house by creating all-glass corner windows. The diagonal view shows the alternating variation in porch structures.

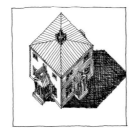

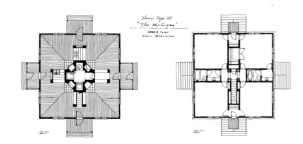

First Floor Plan

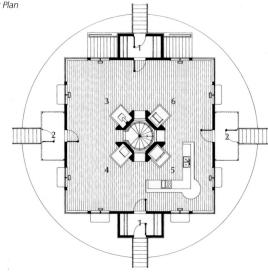

Third Floor Plan

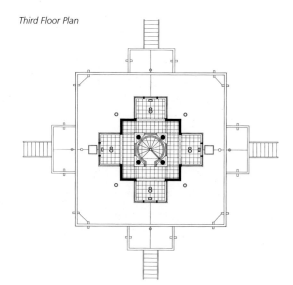

1. Entry

2. Screen Porch

3. Living

4. TV Viewing

5. Kitchen

6. Dining

7. Lookout Retreat

9. Storage

Site Plan

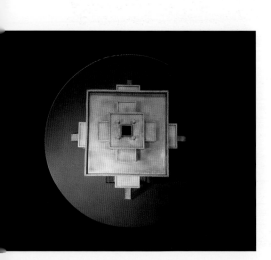

Basement Floor Plan

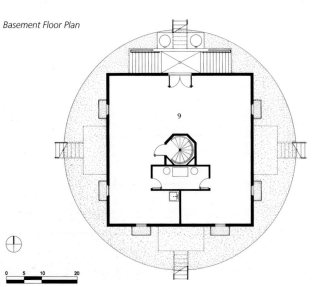

Second Floor Plan

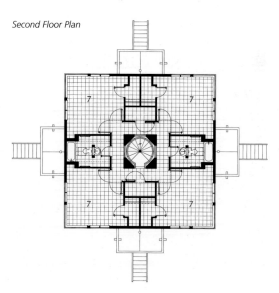

0   5   10   20

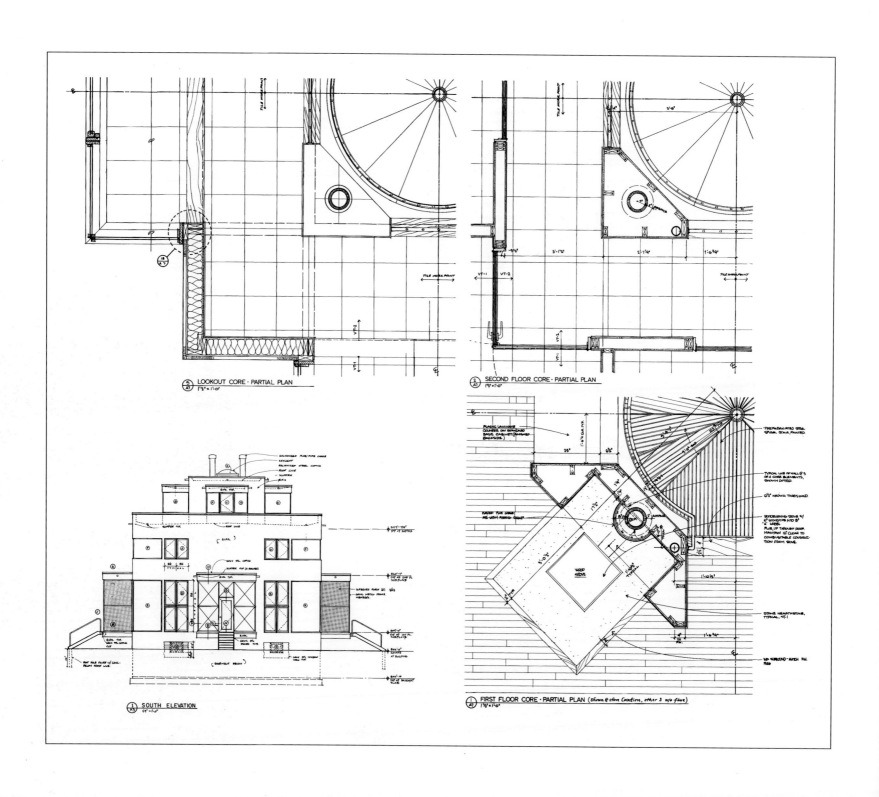

2 LOOKOUT CORE · PARTIAL PLAN
A7   1½" = 1'-0"

3 SECOND FLOOR CORE · PARTIAL PLAN
A7   1½" = 1'-0"

1 SOUTH ELEVATION
A3   ¼" = 1'-0"

1 FIRST FLOOR CORE · PARTIAL PLAN (shown @ stove location, other 3 w/o flue)
A7   1½" = 1'-0"

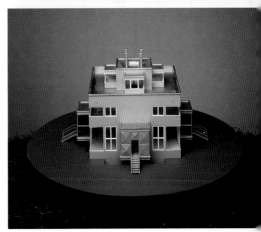

Mussman Residence

Ogden Dunes, Indiana

Having secured a vacant lot on a bluff behind an existing Lake Michigan beach house, a young family initially sought to build a sprawling one-story house. It had to accommodate the parents, their two young children, and a grandmother confined to a wheelchair. Budget constraints required exceptional economy in construction.

To simultaneously take advantage of a cost-effective, compact volume and also maximize extraordinary views envisioned from a higher elevation, the architects developed a three-story scheme that utilized an unconventional arrangement of spaces around a central spine of circulation. Elevated to the third floor, the main living spaces achieve an uninterrupted view of Lake Michigan over the neighboring beach house. The second floor comprises the master suite and two children's bedrooms. The ground floor accommodates the grandmother's apartment and a family room.

To preserve compactness, a three-foot- (one-meter-) wide zone through the center of the house combines the stair, hallway, and lightwell. It contains a straight run stair designed to gradually reveal a view of the lake as one ascends from the entry. The middle landing of the stair serves as a hall with entries to the master suite and bedrooms. Aligned with the stair and matching its width is an overhead skylight that filters daylight through a third-floor aluminum grate and through the open grate stair treads to the ground floor hall below.

1. Entry
2. Recreation
3. In-Law Living
4. In-Law Bedroom
5. Bedroom
6. Sitting
7. Living
8. Dining
9. Kitchen

Third Floor Plan

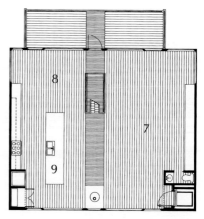

Second Floor Plan

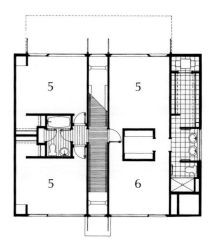

First Floor Plan

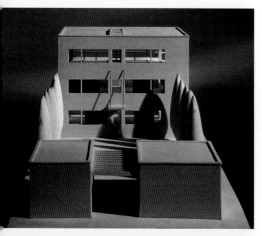

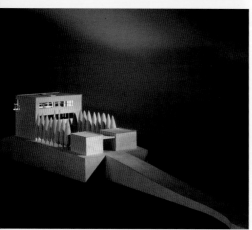

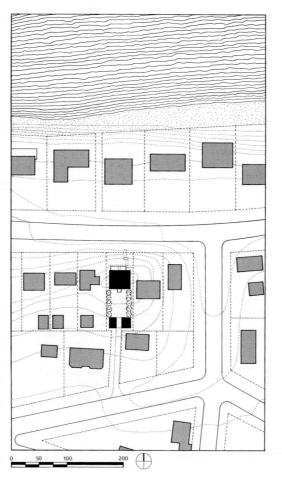

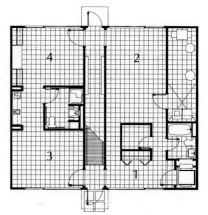

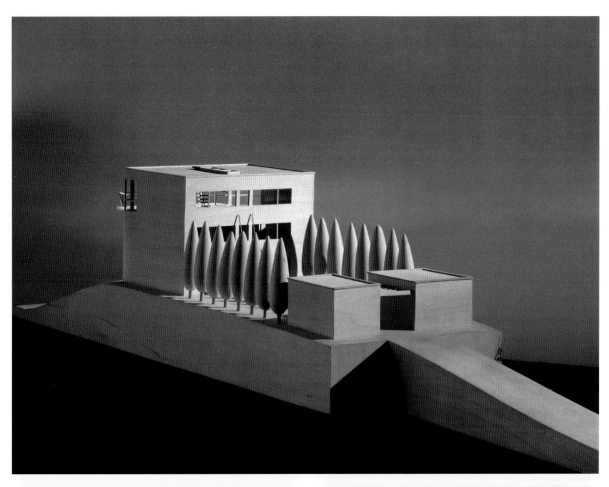

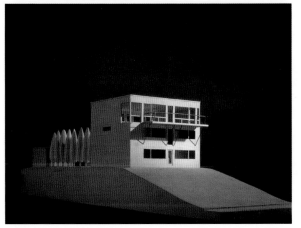

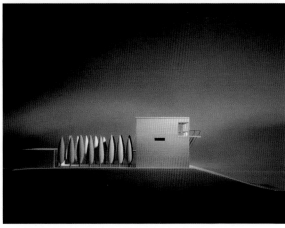

Opposite Page: *The model and site drawings include future garages and a trellis designed to complete the approach sequence to the house.*

Left: *The house sits on the edge of the plateau, with the ground quickly sloping away toward Lake Michigan.*

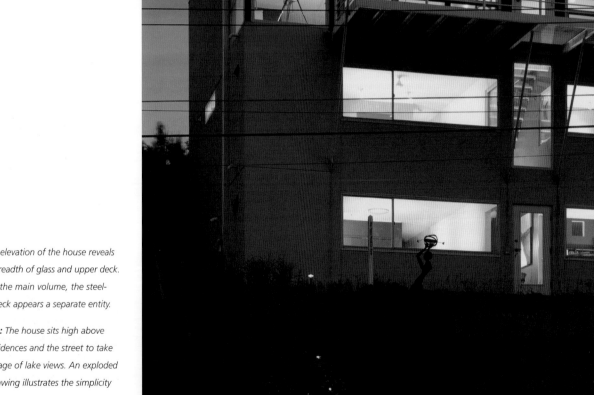

Right: The lake elevation of the house reveals the expanded breadth of glass and upper deck. Detached from the main volume, the steel-framed wood deck appears a separate entity.

Opposite Page: The house sits high above surrounding residences and the street to take the best advantage of lake views. An exploded axonometric drawing illustrates the simplicity of construction.

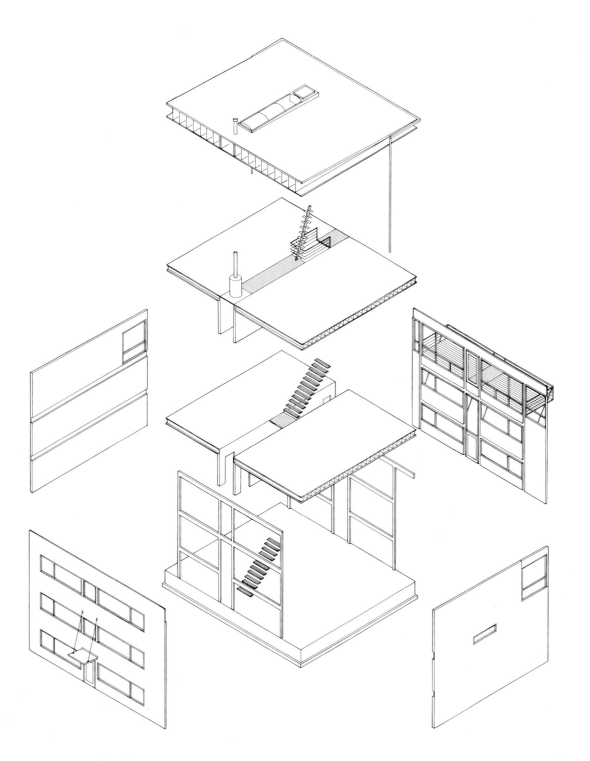

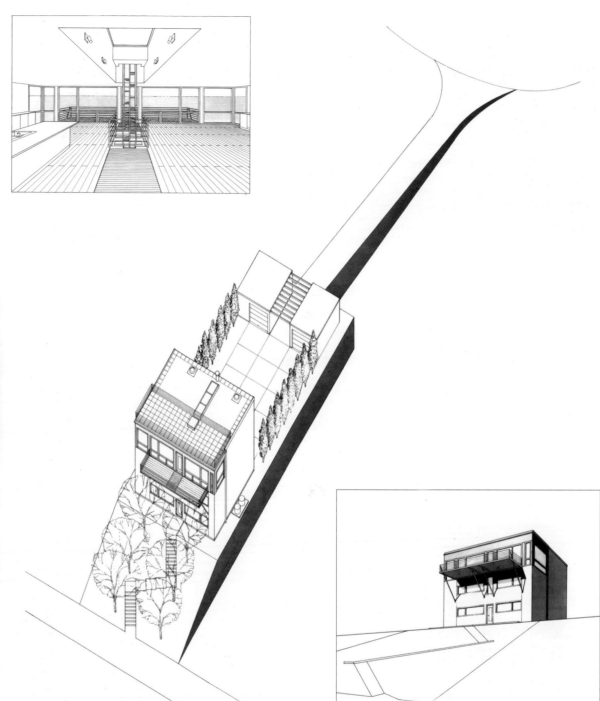

Opposite Page: *A future roof deck expands the upper-level living space in both function and exterior expression. Spartan details at the juncture of dissimilar materials respect the economy of construction while maintaining the design intent.*

Left: *On the courtyard elevation, only the entry canopy punctuates the rigorous exterior skin.*

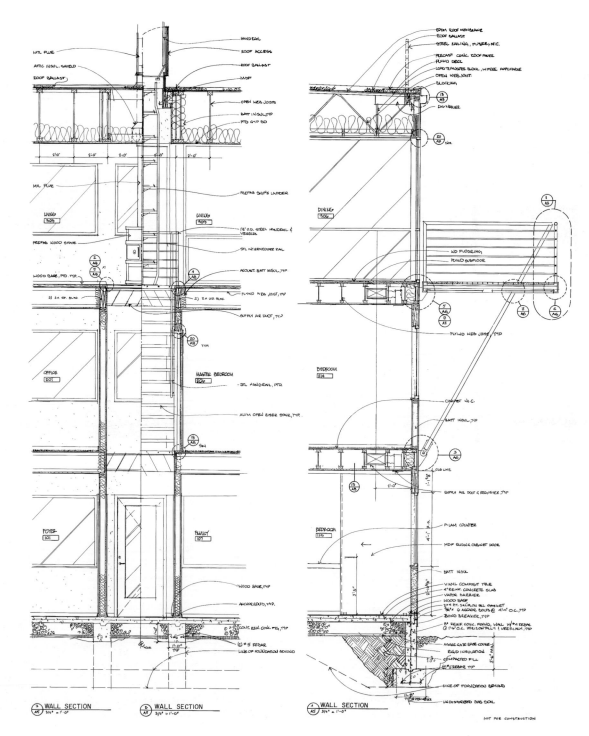

NOT FOR CONSTRUCTION

Opposite Page: The straight-run stair is detailed with available manufactured aluminum grating, joined with an industrial alternating-tread stair to provide rooftop access. Placed with simple and inexpensive details, the common materials assume an uncommon refinement.

Left: A visitor begins at the bottom of the stair feeling slightly confined in a blue-walled cavern. During the ascent, the open riser stair gradually admits more light and more distant views, hinting at what lies at the end of the climb.

Essex Residence and Office

Chicago, Illinois

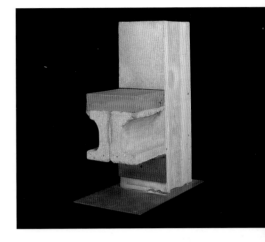

Wheeler Kearns Architects searched with a husband-and-wife graphic design team for an existing building to house their small office and their growing family. Nothing was found within their means, so they looked for land and selected a vacant lot forty-eight feet (fifteen meters) wide on a busy commercial street in the Wicker Park neighborhood. It contained twelve feet (four meters) of buried subsoil debris and zoning required a fire-resistant structure. The scope and program were set within a budget of two-thirds of what one typically could afford.

The architects quickly deemed conventional solutions untenable; with the scope fixed and the understanding that roughly half the cost of construction is material and the other half labor, the only remaining solution was to limit labor on site, hence prefabrication. An exploration of alternatives yielded an industrial pre-cast concrete system typically utilized for warehouses and factories.

__Opposite Page and Left:__ A simple, taut volume capitalizes on the reductive attitude and minimalist aesthetic employed. Insulated-core concrete wall panels isolate the spaces within the building from the noise of its surrounding urban neighborhood. Windows and doors are placed in cadence with these load-bearing panels and integrate with their structural logic.

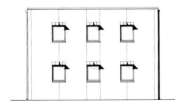

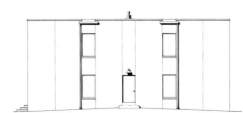

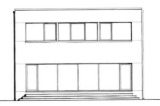

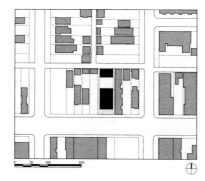

Site Plan

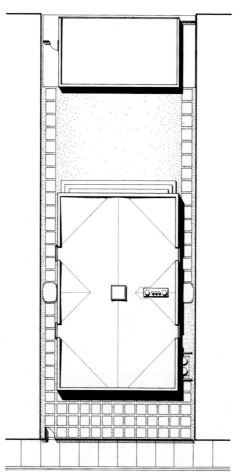

Roof Plan

Second Floor Plan

1. Entry
2. Office Reception
3. Office
4. Work Area
5. Conference
6. Living
7. Dining
8. Kitchen
9. Bedroom
10. Dressing

First Floor Plan

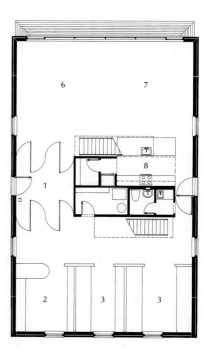

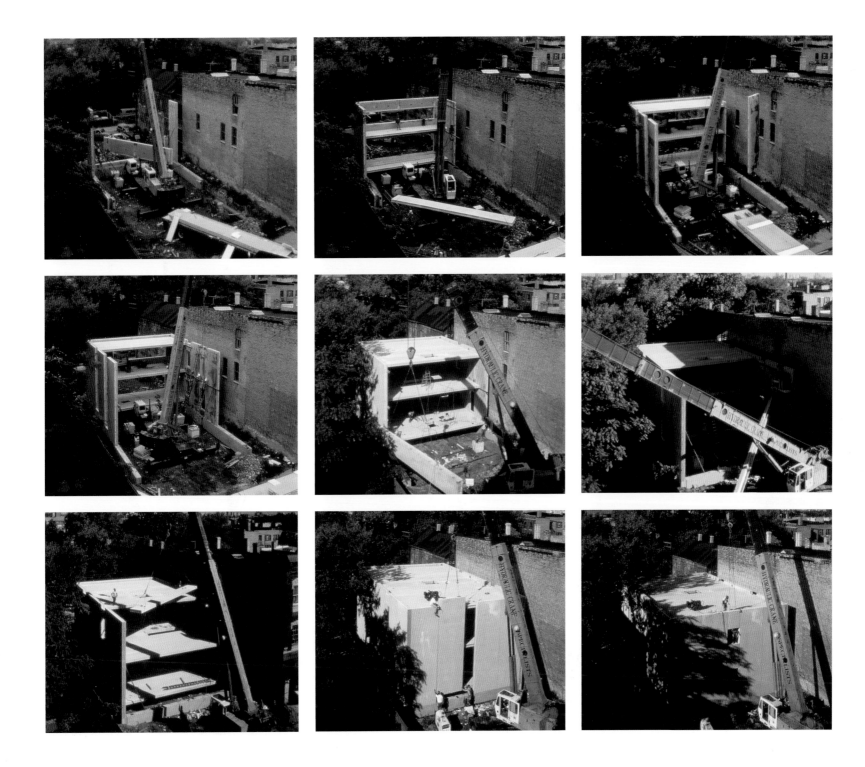

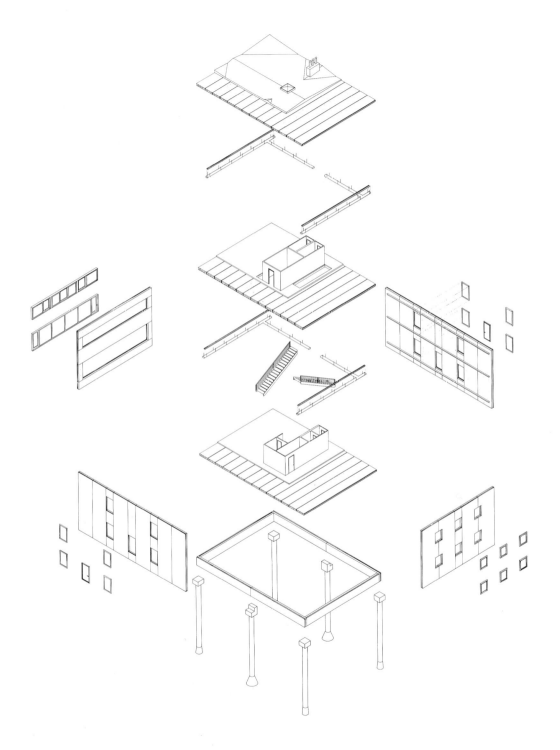

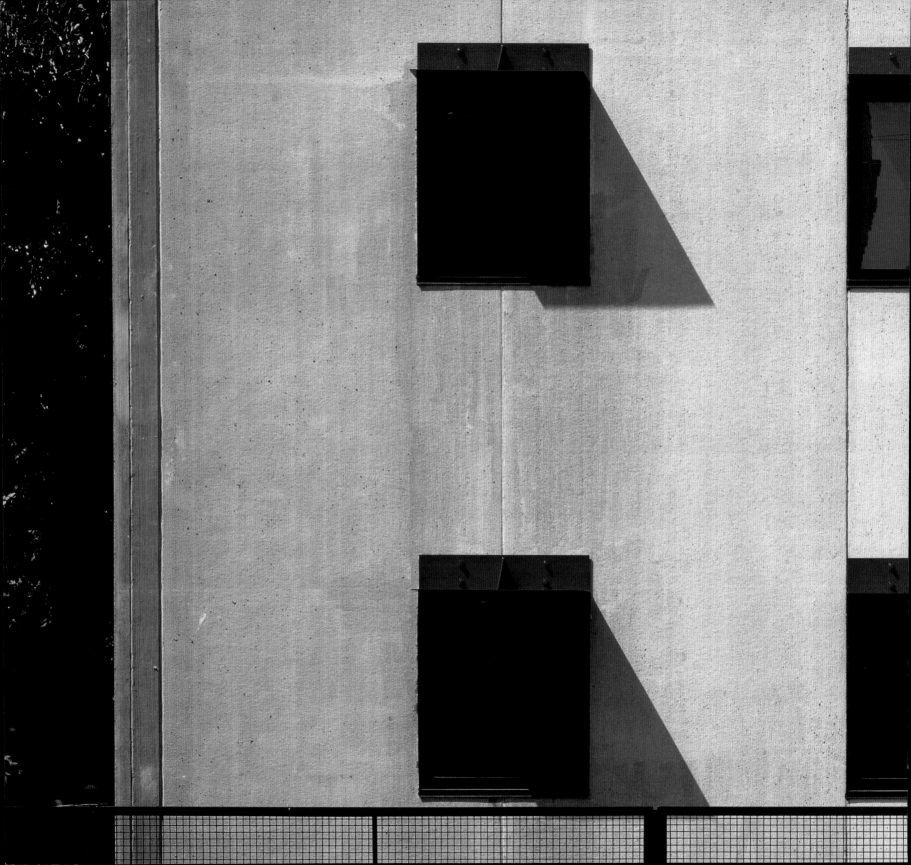

Upon six site-cast caissons, crews erected a prefabricated structure of insulated concrete grade-beams, wall panels, and floor slabs in just four days. Rather than attempting to domesticate the industrial origins of the system, the architects welcomed concrete surfaces and welded plate connections as important facts; a lasting presence of the nature, cadence, and simplicity of the construction. The interior design maintains the straightforward integrity of the materials, yet oiled fiberboard finishes and pigmented concrete floors soften the industrial aesthetic. This building effort consciously questions general assumptions of what a "house" should be and its typically assumed methods of construction. An elegant space of noteworthy permanence, resonance, and integrity has been created within an extremely modest budget.

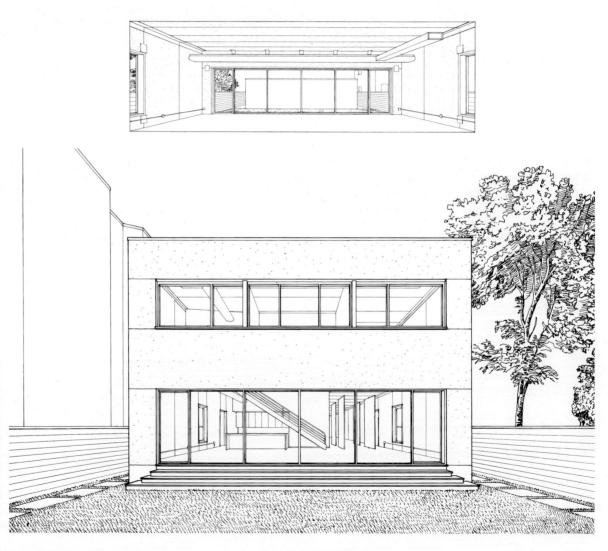

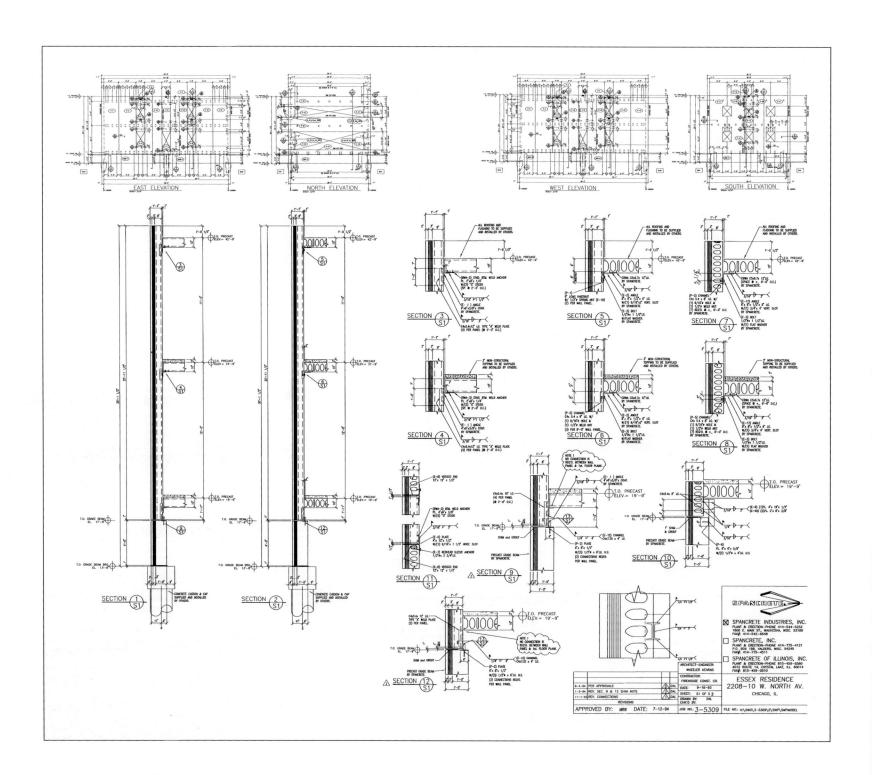

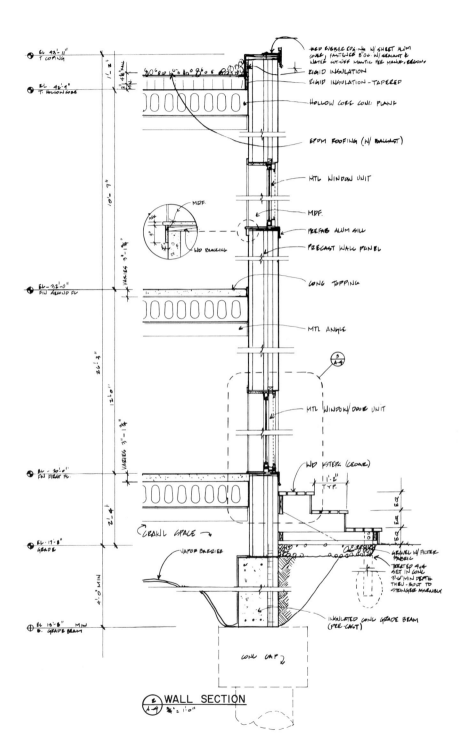

EL 42'-11"
T. COPING

EL 42'-9"
T. HOLLOW CORE

EL 32'-0"
2ND AROUND FLR

EL 20'-0"
FIN FIRST FL

EL 17'-8"
GRADE

EL 13'-8" MIN
B. GRADE BEAM

1'-1"
2'-4 6/8" WALL MIN
10'-9"
VARIES 3'-1 6/8"
22'-9"
12'-0"
VARIES 3'-1 6/8"
2'-4 6/8"
4'-0" MIN

REO RUBBER COPING W/ SHEET ALUM CORE, FASTENED 3'O.C W/ SEALANT & WATER CUT-OFF MASTIC PER MANUF. RECOM.

RIGID INSULATION

RIGID INSULATION - TAPERED

HOLLOW CORE CONC. PLANK

EPDM ROOFING (W/ BALLAST)

MTL WINDOW UNIT

MDF.

MDF.

PREFAB ALUM SILL

PRECAST WALL PANEL

CONC TOPPING

MTL ANGLE

3
A4

MTL WINDOW/DOOR UNIT

WD STEPS (CEDAR)

1'-2"
TYP.

EQ EQ EQ

CRAWL SPACE

VAPOR BARRIER

GRAVEL W/ FILTER FABRIC

THREADED 4x4 SET IN CONC 3'-0" MIN DEPTH THRU-BOLT TO STRINGER ASSEMBLY

INSULATED CONC GRADE BEAM (PRE-CAST)

WD BRACKING

3"

MDF.

CONC CAP'Z

2 **WALL SECTION**
A4   3/4" = 1'-0"

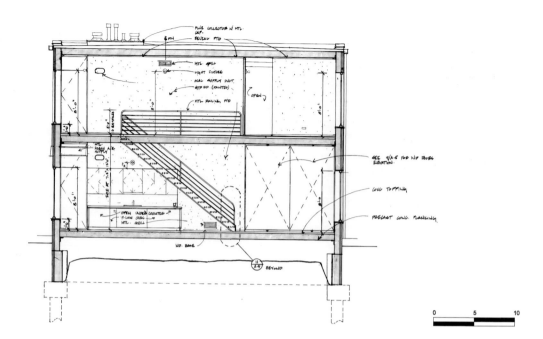

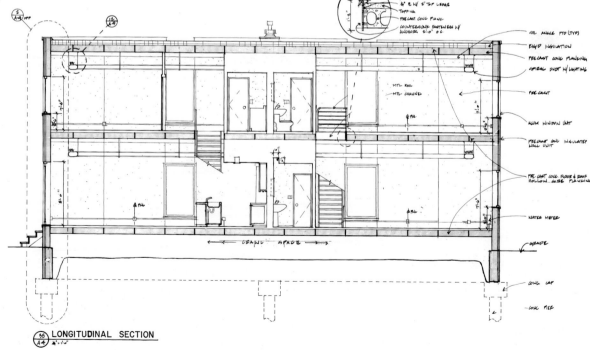

LONGITUDINAL SECTION

Arlington Residence

Chicago, Illinois

A family of five relocating from a ten-acre estate in western Massachusetts purchased this three-flat building in a North Side neighborhood. The challenge of the project was how to capitalize on the narrow lot in the dense neighborhood by maximizing daylight to the interior, views to the exterior, and outside recreation space.

To increase daylight, the architects developed three double-height rooms. These spaces increase in magnitude as one passes from the front of the house to the rear. The first, a music room, lies behind the front facade, modified to combine windows on two floors into a single large opening. A small window seat in the second-floor master suite projects into the double-height space, borrowing light while opening views to the streetscape beyond.

The central double-height space accommodates a dining room flanked by a formal elliptical stair and a two-story window facing an ivy-covered wall. Windows in the second-floor rooms surrounding this space accentuate the sense of transparency throughout the house.

Above: *The steel and glass addition within the private confines of the rear yard exploits a degree of transparency to the exterior environment uncommon for a dense urban site.*

Opposite Page: *Black-painted steel window frames permit the reduction of the exterior wall to a thin framework, maximizing the connection to the outdoors. The space has the characteristic of an outdoor porch, elevated in space, with heightened views of the changing sky.*

1. Maid's Apartment
2. Utility
3. Guest Room
4. Recreation
5. Living
6. Dining
7. Kitchen
8. Family
9. Bedroom
10. Offices
11. Open to Below
12. Terrace
13. Garage
14. Lap Pool

Site Plan

Third Floor

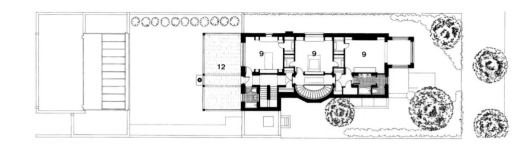

Second Floor

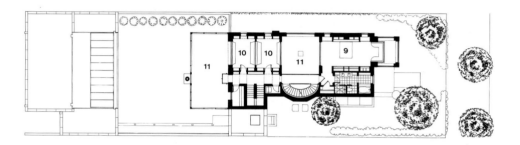

First Floor

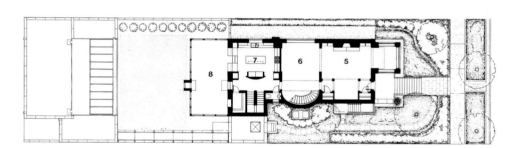

Entry Level

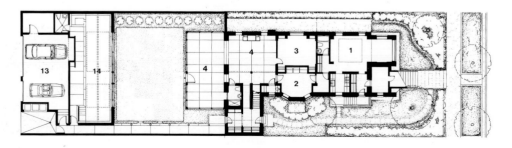

Opposite Page: *The original masonry structure was maintained and adapted as needed. Interior floor and wall framing was completely replaced with new.*

Left: *Modified to combine windows on two floors into a single, large, two-story opening, the front facade is the first of three double-height spaces. New, narrow-profile black steel windows in the opening suggest a degree of transparency that is more fully realized in the rear addition.*

Right: The framework of the family room
addition continues up to the height of the
existing masonry structure, visually tying the
two together and providing a sense of definition for the rooftop terrace and an opportunity
for supporting canopies during the hot summer months.

Opposite Page: The family room fireplace,
cantilevered off the steel and glass structure,
opens to the outside with a clear ceramic glass
panel, capitalizing on the ideas of light structure and transparency.

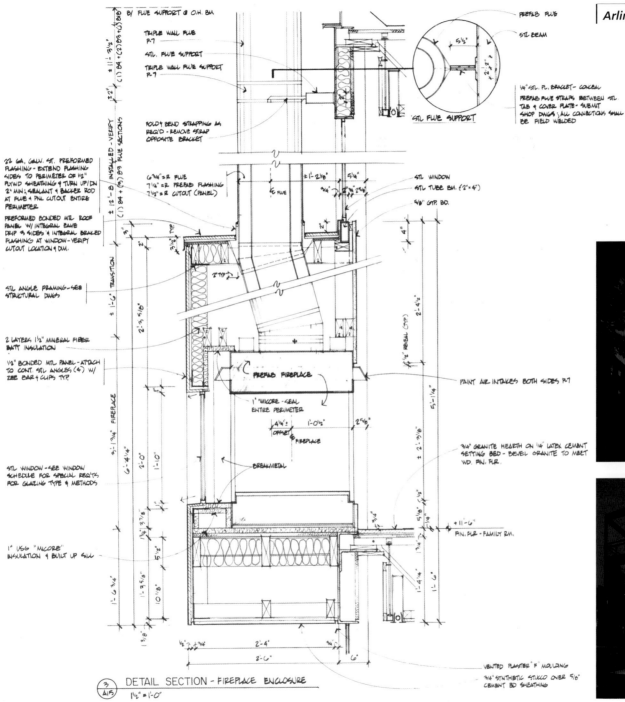

BY FLUE SUPPORT @ O.H. BM

TRIPLE WALL FLUE
R-7

STL. FLUE SUPPORT

TRIPLE WALL FLUE SUPPORT
R-7

FOLD & BEND STRAPPING AS
REQ'D - REMOVE STRAP
OPPOSITE BRACKET

PREFAB FLUE

STL BEAM

'STL FLUE SUPPORT'

1/4" STL. PL. BRACKET - CONCEAL

PREFAB FLUE STRAPS BETWEEN STL
TAB & COVER PLATE - SUBMIT
SHOP DWGS; ALL CONNECTIONS SHALL
BE FIELD WELDED

22 GA. GALV. ST. PREFORMED
FLASHING - EXTEND FLASHING
SIDES TO PERIMETER OF 1/2"
PLYWD SHEATHING & TURN UP/DN
2" MIN; SEALANT & BACKER ROD
AT FLUE & PNL CUTOUT ENTIRE
PERIMETER

6 3/4" = R FLUE
7 1/4" = R PREFAB FLASHING
7 1/2" = R CUTOUT (PANEL)

STL WINDOW

STL TUBE BM. (2" x 4")

5/8" GYP. BD.

PREFORMED BONDED MTL ROOF
PANEL W/ INTEGRAL EAVE
DRIP @ SIDES & INTEGRAL BRAKED
FLASHING AT WINDOW - VERIFY
CUTOUT LOCATION & DIM.

STL ANGLE FRAMING - SEE
STRUCTURAL DWGS

2 LAYERS 1 1/2" MINERAL FIBER
BATT INSULATION

1 1/2" BONDED MTL PANEL - ATTACH
TO CONT. STL ANGLES (4) W/
ZEE BAR & CLIPS TYP.

PREFAB FIREPLACE

1" MCCORE - SEAL
ENTIRE PERIMETER

PAINT AIR INTAKES BOTH SIDES R-7

OFFSET
@ FIREPLACE

3/4" GRANITE HEARTH ON 1/4" LATEX CEMENT
SETTING BED - BEVEL GRANITE TO MEET
WD. FIN. FLR.

STL WINDOW - SEE WINDOW
SCHEDULE FOR SPECIAL REQ'TS
FOR GLAZING TYPE & METHODS

BREAK METAL

FIN. FLR. - FAMILY RM.

1" USG "MCCORE"
INSULATION & BUILT UP SILL

VENTED PLASTER "F" MOULDING

3/4" SYNTHETIC STUCCO OVER 5/8"
CEMENT BD SHEATHING

③
A15

DETAIL SECTION - FIREPLACE ENCLOSURE
1 1/2" = 1'-0"

At the rear, the series of double-height spaces culminates with a spacious glass and steel addition that opens views on three sides. The grade of the rear yard drops eighteen inches (forty-six centimeters) within the confines of the surrounding garden walls, allowing direct access from the lower level. As the center of everyday activity, the first-floor family room enjoys a prominent view of the rear yard while providing light to the kitchen and second floor spaces. To accentuate the transparency of the addition, the fireplace, engaged in the exterior wall, uses clear ceramic glass at the exterior to permit views through it.

At the back of the yard, an enclosed forty-five-foot (fourteen-meter) lap pool shares a wall with the garage. A series of inset double-hung windows visually anchors the structure into the rear garden wall. A continuous skylight affords swimmers a clear view of the sky.

Opposite Page: *The indoor lap pool combines with the garage at the rear of the site. Translucent double-hung windows admit light and air while maintaining privacy. Continuous clear glass skylights provide views of the sky above.*

Left: *A white garden wall defines three sides of the rear yard. The pool structure integrates with the wall, with an architectural language that recalls the steel and glass addition of the main house opposite.*

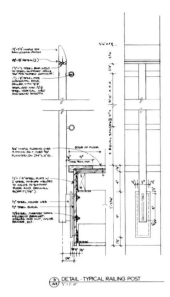

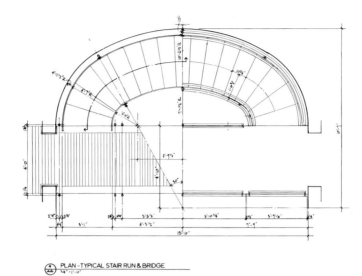

3 DETAIL - TYPICAL RAILING POST
A-4 3" = 1'-0"

4 PLAN - TYPICAL STAIR RUN & BRIDGE
A-4 3/4" = 1'-0"

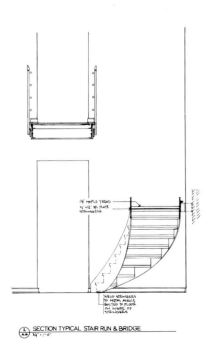

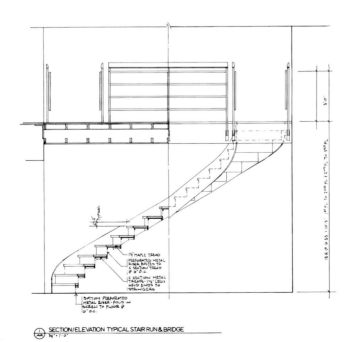

1 SECTION TYPICAL STAIR RUN & BRIDGE
A-4 3/4" = 1'-0"

2 SECTION/ELEVATION TYPICAL STAIR RUN & BRIDGE
A-4 3/4" = 1'-0"

Crosby Residence
Chicago, Illinois

After living in a landmark rowhouse in the city's Near North Side for two years, a graphic designer sought to realize his life-long dream to transform its interior into a museum-caliber series of simple modern spaces. From the outset, the client wanted to develop the interior as a series of floor planes, each rendered with a high-quality material and composed to transcend the sum of its parts.

In order to establish the appropriate character for each of the three levels, each floor plane was constructed of a unique natural material. Paved with British slate, the earthen lower level floor's rich texture and cool colors compliment the existing brick walls. For the formal first level, a quartersawn maple floor sets between the existing plaster walls. A wool carpet woven in a sisal-like pattern completes the private quarters of the upper level.

Gutted in the 1970s, the only interior details that remained of the Victorian-era building were casings and surrounds for the interior elevations of the street facade. These details of the original shell were painstakingly restored as an homage to the original architecture as well as a visual counterpoint to the new interventions.

Above: *The ground-floor entry, partially below grade, acknowledges its immediate contact with the earth through the use of natural slate floors and exposed brick walls. The maple stair treads introduce the flooring material of the more refined first level above.*

Opposite Page: *View from first floor living area, toward dining and kitchen areas. The first-floor level is maintained as a large open volume, with a limited set of new interventions to accommodate the functional needs.*

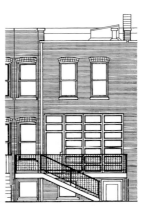

1. Entry
2. Utility
3. Living / Dining
4. Kitchen
5. Bedroom

Second Floor Plan

Site Plan

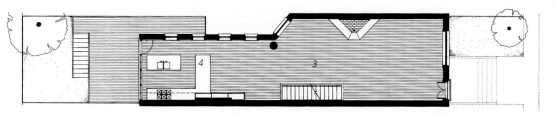

First Floor Plan

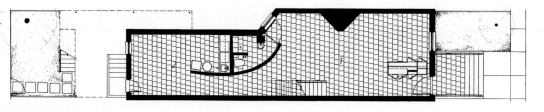

Entry Level

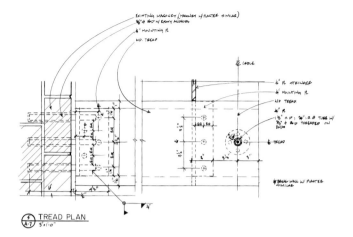

TREAD PLAN

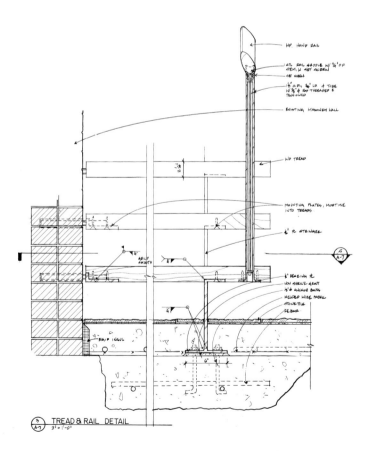

TREAD & RAIL DETAIL

Left: Stair details

Opposite Page: The maple treads, handrails, and stainless-steel-cable stair guards occur on all three levels and serve as reference to all other materials. Stair components are reduced to the essential elements. The masonry wall, eliminating the need for a stringer, individually supports inboard treads. Rail supports and steel plates are mortised into the thick treads and screws are countersunk into the steel for a clean, flush appearance.

Within the remaining shell a series of carefully constructed object-like interventions were inserted that give compositional character and definition to the volume. Each is detailed in a unique material to suit its particular purpose and maintain its discrete identity within the composition. On the first level, these elements include an open, lightweight stair; a vertical plane of ribbon-striped mahogany storage cabinets; a low mass of stainless steel cabinets; and a thin grid of steel and glass window wall.

Representative of the fastidious details of the house, the central stairway is fashioned with individual 2.25-inch- (5.7 -centimeter-) planks of solid maple that float free from the walls, supported by a 0.5-inch- (1.27-centimeter) plate steel stringer mortised flush into the underside of the treads. The inboard ends of the treads are mortised into a thick plate of steel and pinned to the plastered masonry wall, leaving an 0.5-inch (1.27-centimeter) separation between the tread and wall. Supporting the aircraft cable railings, individual stainless steel balusters are bored through the thick maple and threaded to steel sockets mortised into the underside of the treads. The top tread of each flight of the stair sets into the intercepting floor.

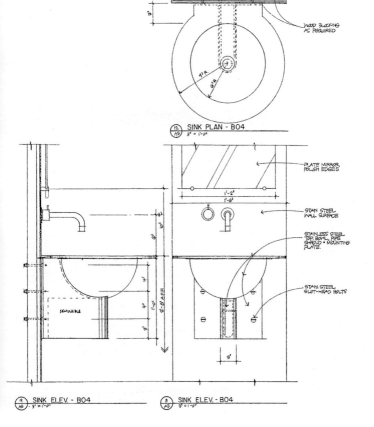

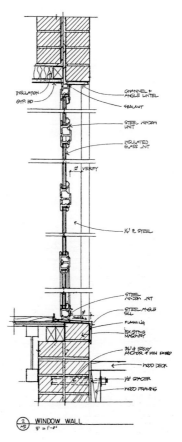

Winnetka Residence

Winnetka, Illinois

This house—designed for a family of five—shows more complexity in its formal relationships than others by Wheeler Kearns; it defies easy diagrammatic description. This is partly attributed to the larger size and subsequently more complex program, and partly to the owners' fairly strict parameters. They sought a continuity between daily living spaces and a variety of outdoor spaces, as well as a maximum utilization of the large rear yard, with its beautiful set of mature trees. Both required an effective use of the one-hundred-by-three-hundred-foot (thirty-by-ninety-meter) site. But most importantly, the design had to achieve a balance between durable materials and human comfort, and any evidence of pretense had to be avoided.

An earlier scheme relied on a set of crisp volumes clearly separated and articulated. It successfully achieved the functional organization the owners sought, but after due consideration was felt to be too formal for the family's needs. At this point emerged the concept for more intimately scaled informal spaces within the larger ones, and a house that slowly unfolds itself to the visitor in a layered progression from public to private. It sought to achieve "the promise of continual surprise." The basic organization of the previous scheme was retained, but it evolved into a more fluid arrangement of space and volume.

Above: Courtyard seen from the family room corner bay. Upholstered window seats contain toy-storage drawers below. The children play in this quiet, protected corner.

Opposite Page: The exterior materials palette includes rough-sawn, random-width, darkly stained cedar, complemented with French limestone paving, naturally weathered gray teak windows, and lead-coated copper standing seam roofs, copings, and downspouts. All are intended to help the mass of the house visually recede into the lushly landscaped site.

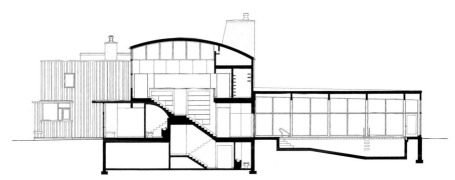

1. Entry
2. Living
3. Study
4. Dining
5. Family
6. Kitchen
7. Pool
8. Garage
9. Bedroom
10. Laundry
11. Loft
12. Open to Below
13. Attic

Site Plan

First Floor Plan

Loft

Basement

Second Floor Plan

Left: *The two-story mass of the main house joins to a one-story service wing by the central stair volume, its intersection capped by a barrel-vaulted roof.*

Opposite Page: *The site plan strategy of creating three distinct landscapes—agreed upon early in the design process—influenced the shaping of the first-floor formal rooms and largely determined the exterior massing and fenestration.*

Right: *The entry hall provides views in multiple directions, including those toward the rear yard and up the front stair to the private spaces of the house. Its warm palette consists of cedar ceilings; Buxy French limestone floors in a random ashlar pattern; and mahogany paneling, window frames, and running trim.*

Opposite Page: *Corners of the first-floor formal spaces are developed as a set of variations on a theme. All offer a common opportunity to pause and view the landscape beyond.*

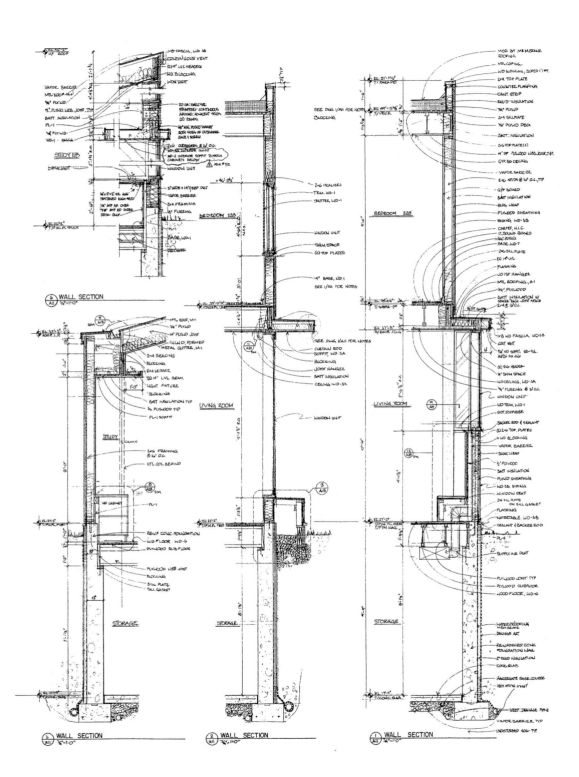

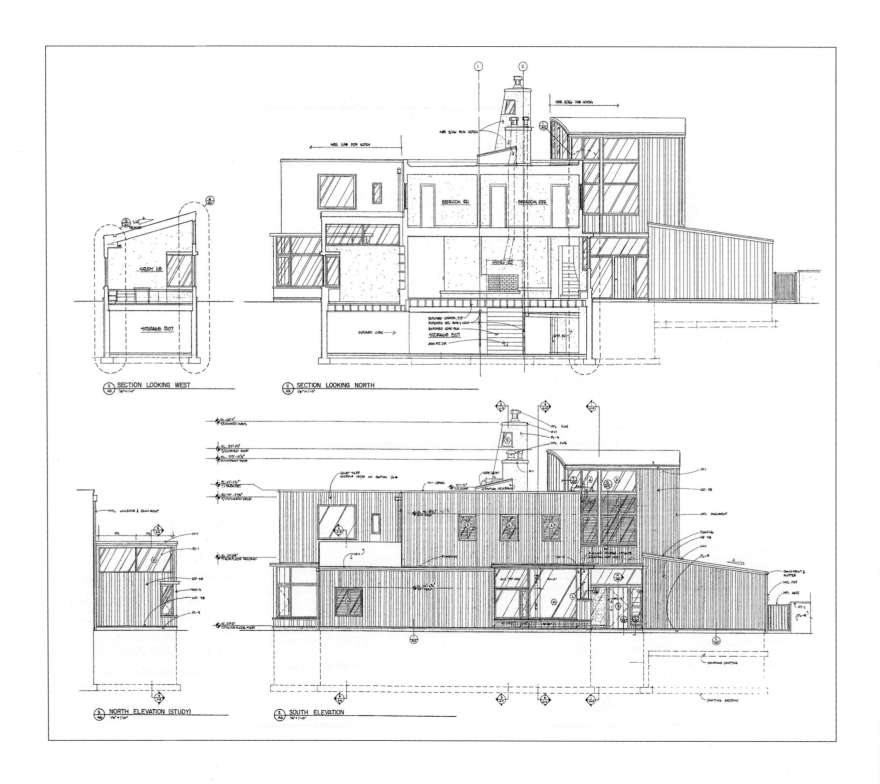

③ SECTION LOOKING WEST

② SECTION LOOKING NORTH

③ NORTH ELEVATION (STUDY)

① SOUTH ELEVATION

Left: *View of the front entry, with the living room bay to the left. Mahogany shutters provide visual privacy; large overhangs toward the south provide relief from the summer sun.*

Opposite Page: *The south entry elevation is organized around the tall stair volume. The concentration of glazing alludes to its role as entry, location of vertical movement and the hinge of the various activities. The overlapping of space apparent in the interior is recalled in the exterior window placement.*

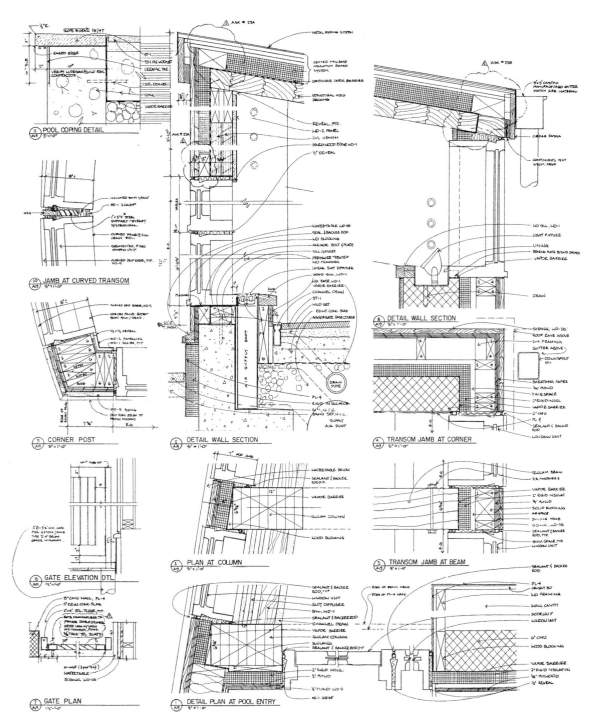

POOL COPING DETAIL

JAMB AT CURVED TRANSOM

CORNER POST

DETAIL WALL SECTION

TRANSOM JAMB AT CORNER

DETAIL WALL SECTION

GATE ELEVATION DTL

PLAN AT COLUMN

TRANSOM JAMB AT BEAM

GATE PLAN

DETAIL PLAN AT POOL ENTRY

The design of the site and house settled around three distinct landscapes: a figural parking and reception court; a central, hidden birch grove; and an expansive open lawn to the rear. The house programmatically divides into two, a wing for living and a wing for support functions. A central stair—itself a combination of two traditional stairs joined at the landing—marks the intersection of the two volumes.

Anchored by masonry fireplace masses, the pinwheel plan defines the different exterior gardens while affording an interior replete with corners. Spaces lead the viewer's gaze diagonally across the width of the rooms and out to the landscapes. The birch tree courtyard, shielded from the approach and entry to the house, is revealed in differing ways at formal areas of the first floor: The living room and study are provided a glancing view to the courtyard, while the dining and family rooms share a broad view, each endowed with a different orientation and scale. As an overall design strategy, particular attention is paid to the corners with the development of quiet sunny bay windows and seats to draw one to each particular place. These well-worn corners, balanced between the interior and exterior environments, encourage a new appreciation of the site's rooms, gardens, and seasons.

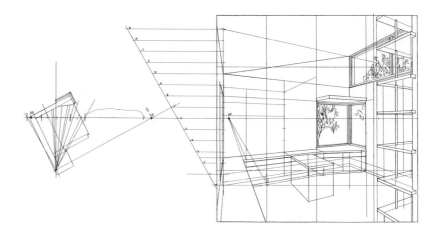

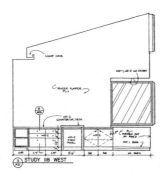

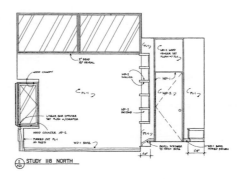

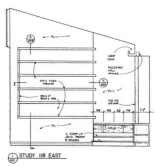

Left: *The primary furniture grouping of the living room (top) centers around the fireplace hearth, complemented by the more intimate, upholstered corner window seat with its views to the garden. Similarly, the generously proportioned kitchen/family room provides a variety of more intimate groupings within the larger volume.*

Opposite Page: *The design process included a series of a dozen one-hour interior perspective sketches of noteworthy spaces, originated during schematic design. Representative of the process is the perspective layout of the private study, and the photograph of the same view.*

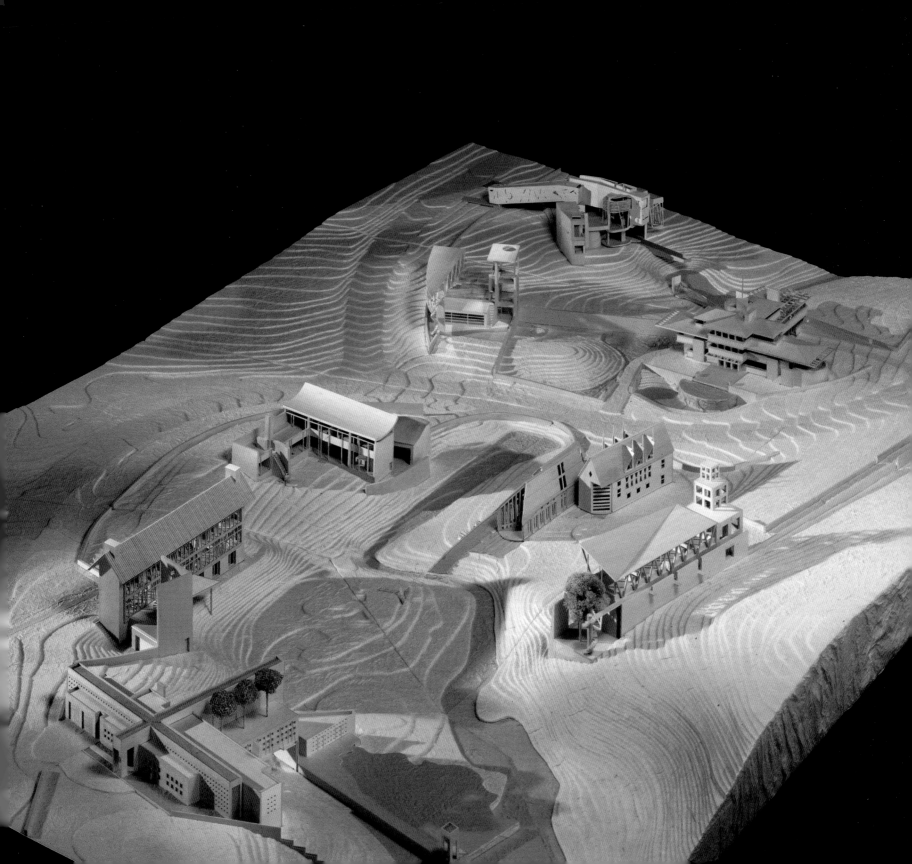

Burr Ridge Residence
Burr Ridge, Illinois

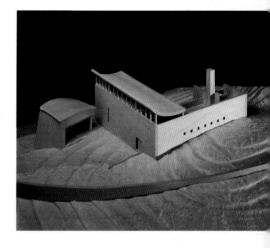

To demonstrate alternative architectural solutions for homes in the area, a Japanese developer invited eight architects to offer designs for a speculative residence sited on a rolling tract of land southwest of Chicago. Typically suburban, large, and uninspired Tudor-style houses on tiny lots surround the area. The heavily wooded site, coupled with relatively small parcels, called for a strategy to best retain its character. Each architect agreed to a size limit of four thousand square feet (372 square meters) and to incorporate a stone wall linking the sites together as a gesture of cooperation and connection to the land.

Wheeler Kearns' L-shaped parti grew directly from the site: solid walls to the north and west, which shield traffic noise and winter winds, and generous glazing to south and east, which face the sun and the creek below. The two wings step to follow the ground plane, settling the house comfortably into the terrain. Mullions placed randomly between the windows produce shadows similar to those of the trees the house replaces. The building's informal, agrarian character is carried within; food preparation and dining are in full view upon entry, with the living space open as well. Each bedroom includes an open bathing area, as a recognition of this integral part of the inhabitants' daily experience.

Above: *The curved surfaces of the garage and main house roof serve as sculptural counterpoints to the disciplined rigor of the north and west enclosing walls.*

Opposite Page: *The eight projects by the following architects, clockwise from top center: Douglas Garofalo, Christopher Rudolph, John Syvertsen, Joseph Valerio, Margaret McCurry, Frederick Phillips, Wheeler Kearns Architects, and Ralph Johnson.*

1. Entry
2. Living
3. Study
4. Kitchen / Dining
5. Bedroom
6. Hall
7. Terrace
8. Carport
9. Utility

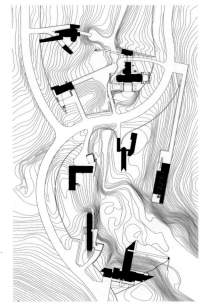

Site Plan

0 50 100   200

0 5 10   20

Cellar Plan   First Floor Plan   Second Floor Plan

Right: Second-floor bathing areas (top) are open to the private bedrooms as recognition of the integral functions of daily existence. Similarly, other interior areas resist physical and functional compartmentalization by maintaining a spatial flow from one to the next.

Opposite Page: Food preparation receives the same attention to detail as other areas, which includes access to light, air, and view. The orientation of the space offers south and east sunlight, and a view across the sloping terrain from all locations.

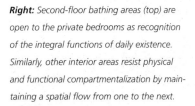

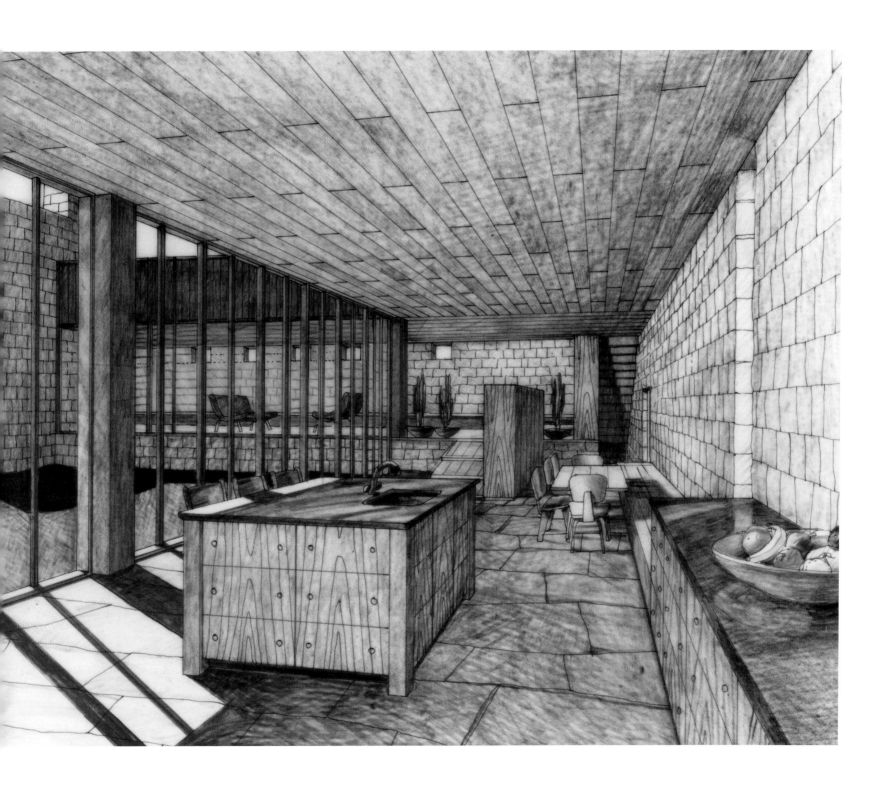

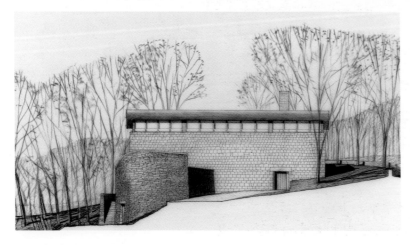
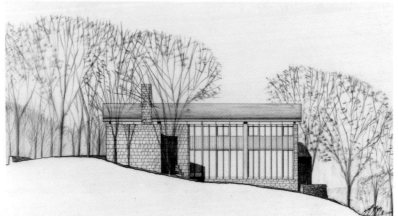

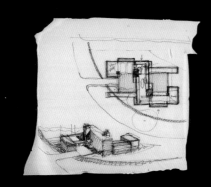
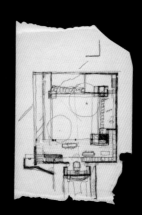

Left: *Early design sketches investigated dual courts with differing functions as well as a single protected courtyard. The four perspective drawings illustrate how the changing sunlight, shown from dawn to dusk, becomes a material participant in the space.*

Opposite Page: *The approach elevation (upper and lower left) consists of massive stone walls, in high contrast to the glass elevations inside of the "L" (upper and lower right).*

Camp Madron Residences

Buchanan Township, Michigan

An abandoned 300-acre (120-hectare) Boy Scout camp in southwestern Michigan was the site of a competition to design a new community of forty-nine homes, each deferring to the rolling wooded landscape. Daniel Wheeler's winning submission reinterpreted simple rural and vernacular typologies, creating three prototypes: the one-room schoolhouse, the cruciform house, and the telescoping house. Shaker architecture, with its simplicity and unity, inspired the massing, constructional philosophy, materials, and techniques. Developed to sit on sites with varied topography, the compact houses each share basic planning principles: large communal spaces—with cooking facilities to encourage communal interaction—and a minimum of two exposures in all rooms, which provide generous ventilation and access to daylight views. Symmetry is the primary compositional tool both inside and out. While differing in program, each house shares common details, materials, and the implicit character that is evoked from this rigor.

The houses break from outward convention in subtle ways. Plywood stress skins make possible corner windows, which maximize vistas from the interior uncommon in rural prototypes. Metal fireplaces cantilevered from the house structure help keep costs down. On the whole, the houses are planned and built simply, to wear hard and well.

Above: *The lodge offers communal facilities and sustenance to residents and visitors alike.*

Opposite Page: *House 2 maintains a compact footprint and sits within the heavily wooded terrain.*

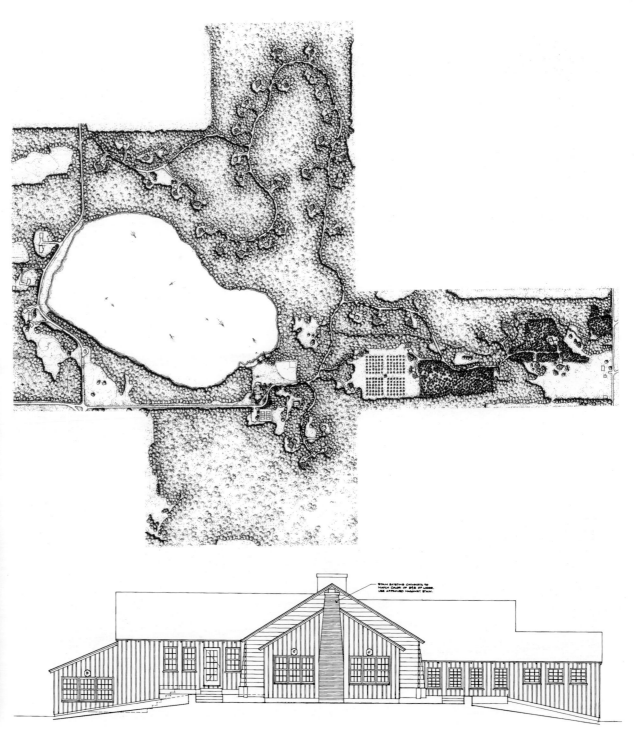

Opposite Page and Left: *The renovation of the existing timbered lodge recaptures the spirit of the original Camp Madron. Centrally located near the lake, it contains a common great hall, library, dining room, game rooms, and kitchen.*

Next Spread: *House 1, the smallest of the designs, comprises essentially one room but shares much of its character with the larger houses. A voluminous interior—made possible by steel collar tie rods that eliminate the typical wood truss and convert a structural necessity to a thoughtful detail—counters its apparent small size from the exterior.*

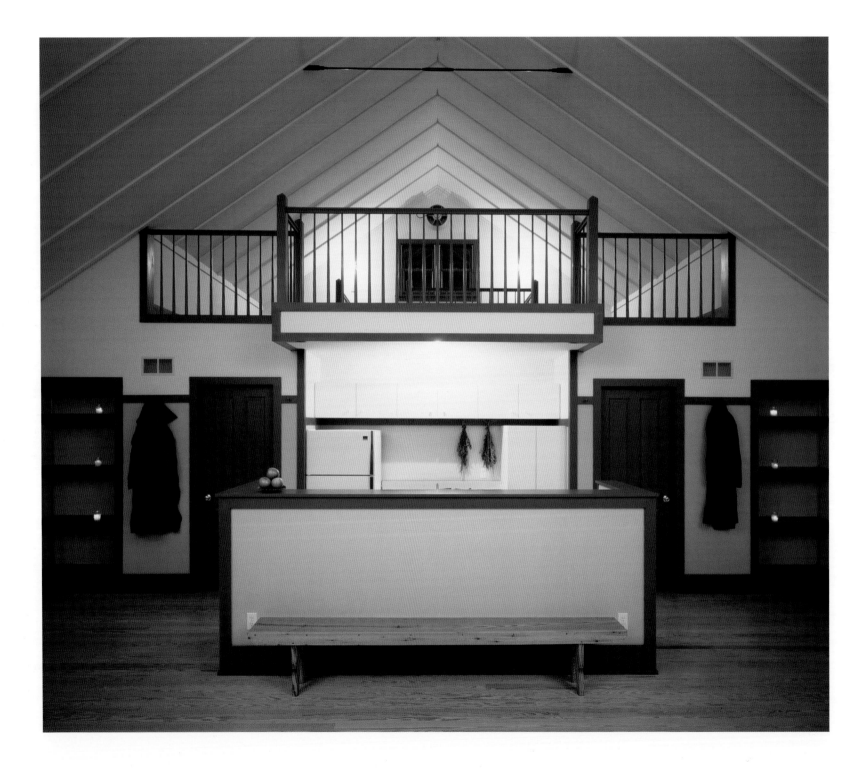

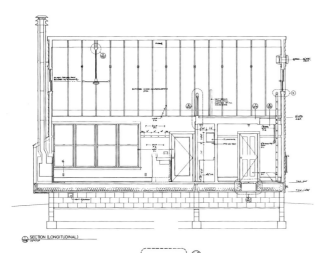

SECTION (LONGITUDINAL)

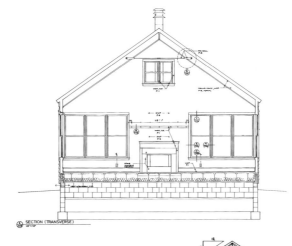

SECTION (TRANSVERSE)

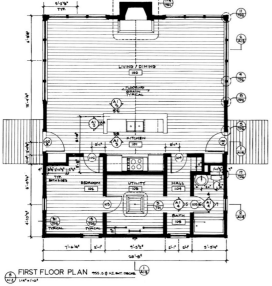

FIRST FLOOR PLAN

LOFT LEVEL PLAN

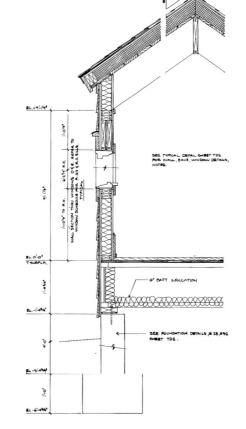

BUILDING SECTION

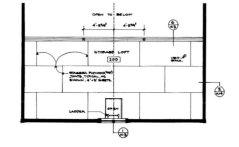

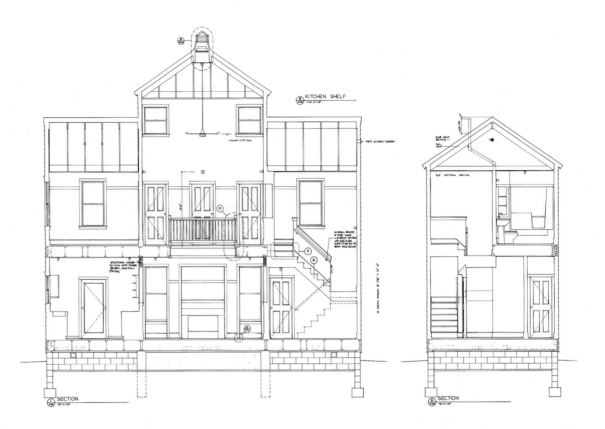

KITCHEN SHELF

SECTION

SECTION

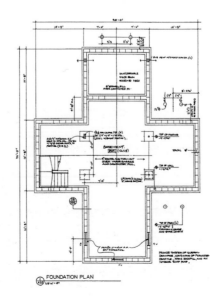

FOUNDATION PLAN

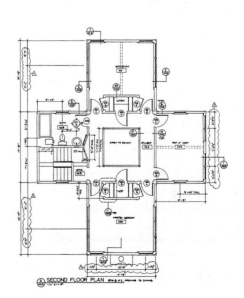

SECOND FLOOR PLAN

Previous Spread: *House 2 adopts a cruciform plan that affords generous light and cross-ventilation to all spaces. Dining, by virtue of its encouragement of communal gathering, is placed at the center, with all other activities extending out from its central position.*

Opposite Page and Right: *House 3 utilizes a telescoping mass in multiple directions to accommodate the most complex program. Economy of means and simplicity of detail are maintained. Peg rails, window trim, and tall baseboards are unadorned and functional throughout.*

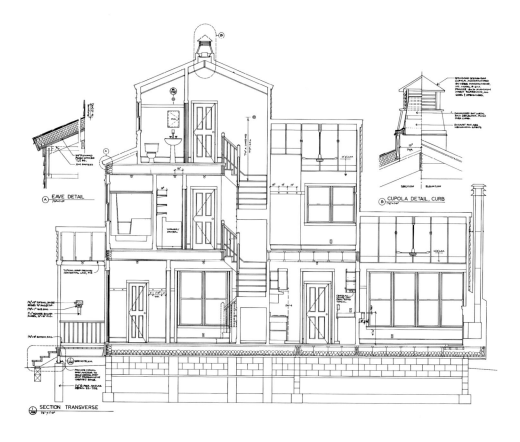

Ⓐ EAVE DETAIL

Ⓑ CUPOLA DETAIL, CURB

SECTION TRANSVERSE

FIRST FLOOR (M.E.P)

SECOND FLOOR (M.E.P)

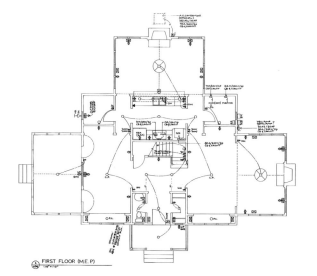

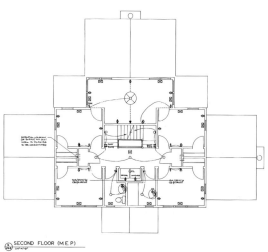

Selected Buildings and Projects

Essex Residence and Office

Chicago, Illinois

Consultants: LeMessurier Consultants, Inc. (structural)

General Contractor: Firehouse Construction

Lot Size: 6,250 sf (580 sm)

Building Size: 4,400 sf (410 sm)

Date of Design: 1993

Construction Completion: 1995

Winnetka Residence

Winnetka, Illinois

Consultants: Leslie Jones Interiors, Inc. (finishes & furnishings); Stearn Joglekar, Ltd. (structural)

General Contractor: The Meyne Company

Lot Size: 1 acre (0.4 ha)

Building Size: 10,200 sf (950 sm)

Date of Design: 1991–1992

Construction Completion 1993

Bohan Kemp Residence

Buchanan Township, Michigan

Consultants: TT-CBM Engineers (structural)

General Contractor: Mead Construction

Lot Size: 0.5 acre (0.2 ha)

Building Size: 1,900 sf (180 sm)

Date of Design: 1996

Construction Completion: 1998

Michigan Residence

Buchanan Township, Michigan

Consultants: Stearn Joglekar, Ltd (structural)

General Contractor: N/A

Lot Size: 0.5 acre (0.2 ha)

Building Size: 4,000 sf (370 sm)

Date of Design: 1989

Construction Completion: Project

Arlington Residence

Chicago, Illinois

Consultants: Powell Kleinschmidt (interior finishes and furnishings)

General Contractor: The Kissner Company

Lot Size: 8,750 sf (810 sm)

Building Size: 9,200 sf (850 sm)

Date of Design: 1988

Construction Completion: 1990

Burr Ridge Residence

Burr Ridge, Illlinois

Developer/Client: Pacific Sakata Corporation

Lot Size: 0.75 acre (0.3 ha)

Building Size: 4,000 sf (370 sm)

Date of Design: 1991

Construction Completion: N/A

LaPoint Residence

Buchanan Township, Michigan

Consultants: Stearn Joglekar, Ltd (structural)

General Contractor: Elder Jones Construction

Lot Size: 0.5 acre (0.2 ha)

Building Size: 3,100 sf (290 sm)

Date of Design: 1989–90

Construction Completion: 1990

Mussman Residence

Ogden Dunes, Indiana

Consultants: Stearn Joglekar, Ltd (structural)

General Contractor: Michigan City Associates

Lot Size: 8,100 sf (750 sm)

Building Size: 3,750 sf (350 sm)

Date of Design: 1991

Construction Completion: 1992

Crosby Residence

Chicago, Illinois

Consultants: N/A

General Contractor: H & R Johnson Brothers

Lot Size: 1,800 sf (170 sm)

Building Size: 3,000 sf (280 sm)

Date of Design: 1993–1996

Construction Completion: 1997

Camp Madron Residences,

Buchanan Township, Michigan

Consultants: Howard Stearn (structural); Mid-Continent Engineering (mechanical)

General Contractor: Superior Builders

Lot Size: 0.5 acre (0.2 ha)

Building Size: 1,300 sf (120 sm), 1,800 sf (170 sm), and 300 sf (28 sm)

Date of Design: 1987–1988

Construction Completion: 1989

Wheeler Kearns Architects

1987–1999

Daniel Wheeler, FAIA

Lawrence Kearns, AIA

Thomas Bader, AIA

Suzanne Auerbach

John Eck

Joy Meek

Mark Spencer

Mark Weber

Julie Rivkin Wheeler

Contributing Colleagues

John Arzarian

Liza Bachrach

Mark Bastion

Alexander Berghausen

Stefan Browning

Aaron Bruckerhoff

John Cronin

Joel Dankoff

Daniella Dreher

Brad Erdy

Lorenzo Felder

Barbara Felix

Dominique Herison-LaPlae

Phil Keller

Ryan Kennihan

Daniel Marshall

Megan Moore

Frank Mullen

Anne Paas

Amanda Williams

establishing his own private practice in Chicago. Six months later, a former colleague, Lawrence Kearns, joined him to form Wheeler Kearns Architects. They began laying the philosophical groundwork that would guide the firm's process as well as product.

The process, coined as a "collective practice," contributes greatly to the success of this small firm. In its current form, eight full-time, registered architects equally share the roles of designer, technician, and project manager. Each project has a coordinating architect, but everyone has a voice in the design criticism of each project. Everyone works in an open studio. Everyone is closely connected to the conception, modeling and detailing of each project. This non-hierarchical and participatory atmosphere extends equally to encompass the role of owners, consultants, and builders alike.

While their body of work varies greatly, it is driven by a search for the "simple solution," considered the most elusive, seductive, and lyrical aspect of architecture at Wheeler Kearns Architects. The firm eschews a signature style in favor of this abstract notion that transcends stylistic responses.

To continue in the pursuit of their goals, Wheeler Kearns Architects seeks out small- to medium-sized projects with intellectually challenging programs and involved clients. The firm enjoys these projects, typically institutional or residential, because they best utilize its talents and coincide with established goals. Speculative projects for anonymous users are considered problematic and are approached with utmost caution.

Holding fast to this groundwork has proved valuable as Wheeler Kearns Architects has gained recognition. Early notice for its residential work in 1989 by the AIA's Chicago Chapter was followed in 1992 by the AIA's national publication, *Architecture* when it included Wheeler Kearns Architects in their list of nine national firms of "emerging talent." Owing considerably to the principals'

ideas about group practice, Wheeler Kearns Architects was again recognized in 1996 by a national jury for the Chicago Firm Award, typically bestowed upon larger, well-established firms. Their work has been exhibited and published in the United States and abroad. The office has cooperatively taught undergraduate and graduate architecture studios at The University of Illinois at Chicago; various individual members maintain an ongoing teaching, visiting critic, and juror schedule.

Besides the residential projects presented here, other noteworthy projects by Wheeler Kearns Architects include The Chicago Children's Museum, master plan and building design for a large corporate headquarters in North Dakota, several school renovations and additions, and numerous high-rise residential apartments. Current work includes the internationally renowned Old Town School of Folk Music in Chicago, renovation design for a large retail and commercial loft building on Chicago's waterfront, and design for the prominent North Avenue Beach House for Chicago's Public Building Commission. The firm operates a Website at [http://wkarch.com] that not only distributes project information among consultants and clients, but also has portions open to the general public and is periodically updated.

Special thanks to Tom Beeby for his contribution of the introduction, Oscar Riera Ojeda for his constant attention to detail, and all our family members, friends, teachers, peers, and clients for their support over the years.

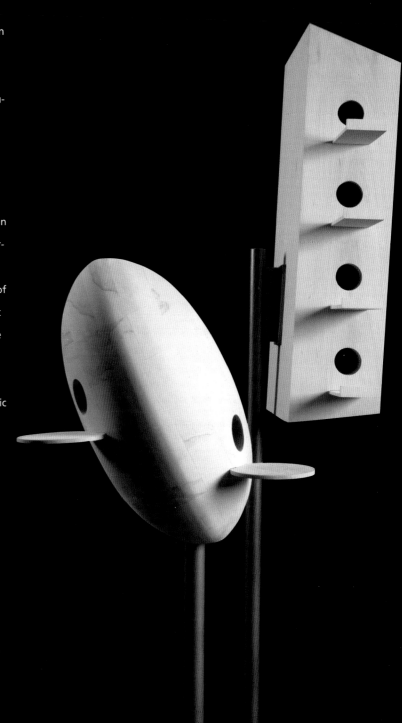

Opposite Page: *Daniel Wheeler Julie Wheeler Suzanne Auerbach John Eck Tom Bader Lawrence Kearns Mark Spencer Mark Weber*
Right: *Birdhouse. 1993*
Previous Spread: *Roach/Eimer Residence, Chicago, Illinois. 1992*

Steve Hall © Hedrich Blessing
Astor Street Residence p.13 (right)

Mark Joseph Photography
Essex Residence and Office p. 56, 67 (bottom), p. 68 (bottom)

Barbara Karant, Karant & Associates Inc.
Winnetka Residence pp. 88, 95, 100

William Kildow Photography
Wine Merchant's Studio pp. 8, 9
Fullerton Residence p. 10
Harrington Residence p. 11
Conceptual Translucent Screen p. 12, 13 (left)
Wilson Painting Studio p. 14
Bohan Kemp Residence
LaPoint Residence
Michigan Residence
Mussman Residence
Essex Residence and Office
Arlington Residence
Crosby Residence
Winnetka Residence
Camp Madron Residences

George Lambros, Lambros Photography
Seminary Residences p.15
Mussman Residence pp. 2, 48, 50 (bottom), 51, 54, 55

James Steinkamp © Steinkamp/Ballogg Chicago
Mussman Residence (model shots)
Winnetka Residence (model shots)
Burr Ridge (model shots)

Wheeler Kearns Architects
LaPoint Residence pp. 27, 28, 29
Mussman Residence pp. 45, 49
Essex Residence and Office p. 58